PETITE
Treats

PETITE Treats

Mini Versions of Your Favorite Baked Delights

MORGAN GREENSETH and CHRISTY BEAVER

Ulysses Press

Published by: Ulysses Press
      P.O. Box 3440
      Berkeley, CA 94703
      www.ulyssespress.com

ISBN: 978-1-61243-111-6
Library of Congress Catalog Number 2012940429

Printed in the United States by Bang Printing

10 9 8 7 6 5 4 3 2 1

Acquisitions editor: Kelly Reed
Managing editor: Claire Chun
Editor: Lauren Harrison
Proofreader: Elyce Berrigan-Dunlop
Production: Jake Flaherty
Interior photographs: featured recipes © www.judiswinksphotography.com; all other photos from shutterstock.com: p. 13 © Suslik1983; p. 18 © Nattika; p. 25 © Garsya; p. 35 © rebvt; p. 49 © Sergey Kotenev; p. 64 © Diana Taliun; p. 73 © by Nadiia Ishchenko; p. 95 © photolinc; p. 100 © Hysteria; p. 105 © Valery121283; p. 107 © Angel Simon; p. 111 © Preto Perola; p. 122 © Kovalchuk Oleksandr; p. 133 © lenetstan
Cover photographs: © www.judiswinksphotography.com

Distributed by Publishers Group West

To the dedicated fans of Mini Empire,
who are helping us take over the world,
one tiny dessert at a time.

TABLE OF CONTENTS

CLASSIC BITES

FANCY STUFF

FROSTINGS, FILLINGS, TOPPINGS, AND DRIZZLES

INTRODUCTION

Miniatures make everything better! We LOVE sweet treats, and we love making them smaller. We showed you how to miniaturize the pie in our first book, *Mini Pies*. Now we move on to exciting new adventures in the world of mini.

This adorable little book contains a broad spectrum of desserts perfect for holidays, birthdays, or any old day. We've made this innovative deliciousness approachable and completely possible for even a novice baker. Start with the donuts and brownies, then work your way up to the fancy stuff like the granddaddy mini dessert of them all, the Piecaken. Before you know it, you'll be a total pro and the adorable hero of every party.

Everyone has a sweet spot, and with this book you can create a portion for every palate. Remember: Don't diet, miniaturize it!

Sweetest regards,
Christy Beaver and
Morgan Greenseth

MORNING BITES

Get your day off to a delicious start. You can't have anything but a good day when it begins with a zesty mini coffee cake, a sweet bitty bun, or a mini morning glory muffin. Great for breakfast gatherings or a quiet Sunday at home, these little treats will ensure that you have a good morning.

BANANA-BLUEBERRY MUFFINS

No need to decide. Combine two of the classics. MAKES 24

1 cup sugar

2¼ cups all-purpose flour

1 teaspoon baking powder

1 teaspoon baking soda

¼ teaspoon salt

3 ripe medium bananas

1 large egg, at room temperature

½ cup (1 stick) unsalted butter,
   at room temperature

½ teaspoon vanilla extract

1½ cups blueberries, fresh or frozen

1. Preheat the oven to 350°F. Line 24 mini muffin wells with paper liners.

2. Sift together the sugar, flour, baking powder, baking soda, and salt.

3. In an electric mixer fitted with the paddle attachment, beat the bananas on low until mashed. Increase the speed to medium. Add the egg, butter, and vanilla. Mix until combined.

4. Gradually add the flour mixture on medium speed until combined.

5. Reduce the speed to low and add the blueberries. Mix briefly until blueberries are evenly distributed.

6. Using a 1-inch ice cream scoop, fill each muffin liner to just below the brim.

7. Bake until the tops are lightly browned, 20 to 22 minutes, rotating the pan halfway through.

8. Allow to cool for 5 minutes in the pan, or until safe to handle. Then transfer to cooling racks to cool completely.

9. Store in an airtight container for up to 2 days.

FROSTED APPLE SPICE MUFFINS

Like a cup of hot cider in your hand. MAKES 18

FOR THE MUFFINS:

1 cup all-purpose flour

½ teaspoon baking soda

½ teaspoon salt

1 teaspoon ground cinnamon

½ teaspoon ground nutmeg

¼ teaspoon ground allspice

⅛ teaspoon ground cloves

¼ cup (½ stick) unsalted butter,
   at room temperature

½ cup granulated sugar

¼ cup brown sugar, packed

2 large eggs

¾ cup unsweetened applesauce

½ cup chopped walnuts

FOR THE FROSTING:

¼ cup (½ stick) unsalted butter,
   at room temperature

4 ounces cream cheese, softened

2 teaspoons sugar

1 teaspoon ground cinnamon

MAKE THE MUFFINS:

1. Preheat the oven to 350°F. Line 18 mini muffin wells with paper liners.

2. Whisk together the flour, baking soda, salt, cinnamon, nutmeg, allspice, and cloves in a medium bowl.

3. Place the butter, granulated sugar, and brown sugar in the bowl of an electric mixer fitted with the paddle attachment. Beat on medium speed until pale and fluffy, about 3 minutes.

4. Add the eggs one at a time, scraping down the bowl as needed. Reduce the speed to low and add the applesauce. Gradually add the flour mixture until combined. Stir in the walnuts by hand.

5. Using a 1-inch ice cream scoop and heaping portions, fill each mini muffin liner to the brim.

SWEET TIPS: *The frosting is only slightly sweet, to allow the flavor of the muffins to shine like the morning sun.*

6. Bake until lightly browned and a toothpick inserted into the center returns with no crumbs, about 20 minutes, rotating the pan halfway through. Allow to cool 5 minutes in the pan, or until safe to handle. Then transfer to cooling racks to cool completely.

MAKE THE FROSTING:

1. While the muffins are baking, combine the butter, cream cheese, sugar, and cinnamon in an electric mixer fitted with the paddle attachment. Beat on medium speed until combined, about 3 minutes.

2. Transfer the frosting into a pastry bag and refrigerate.

3. When the muffins have completely cooled, frost each one.

4. Refrigerate in an airtight container for up to 3 days.

MORNING GLORY MUFFINS

We think you can judge a bakery by its Morning Glories. And these are freaking fantastic.   MAKES 24

⅔ cup sugar

1¼ cups all-purpose flour

½ tablespoon ground cinnamon

1 teaspoon baking soda

¼ teaspoon salt

¼ cup shredded sweetened coconut

½ cup currants

½ cup peeled grated apple
(we like Granny Smith)

½ cup drained crushed pineapple

1 cup shredded carrots

¼ cup chopped walnuts

1½ large eggs

½ cup vegetable oil

½ teaspoon vanilla extract

1. Preheat the oven to 350°F. Spray 24 mini muffin wells with cooking spray or line them with paper liners.

2. Combine the sugar, flour, cinnamon, baking soda, salt, coconut, currants, apple, pineapple, carrots, and walnuts in a large bowl.

3. In a medium bowl, whisk the eggs, oil, and vanilla.

4. Add the wet ingredients to the dry ingredients and mix with a spatula.

5. Fill the muffin wells to the brim using a 1-inch ice cream scoop.

6. Bake until a toothpick inserted in the center returns with no crumbs, about 25 minutes, rotating the pan halfway through.

7. Allow to cool 5 minutes in the pan, or until safe to handle. Then transfer to cooling racks to cool completely.

8. Store in an airtight container for up to 2 days.

PUMPKIN SPICE SCOOKIES WITH FALL SPICE GLAZE

Who said pumpkins were just for pie? MAKES 16

1⅓ cups all-purpose flour

¼ cup granulated sugar, plus more for sprinkling

1½ tablespoons brown sugar

¾ tablespoon baking powder

½ teaspoon ground cinnamon

½ teaspoon ground nutmeg

½ teaspoon ground ginger

¼ teaspoon ground cloves

¼ cup (½ stick) very cold unsalted butter, cut to ¼-inch cubes

⅓ cup pure canned pumpkin

5 tablespoons heavy whipping cream

1 large egg

1 recipe Fall Spice Glaze (page 136)

1. Preheat the oven to 425°F and butter a mini scone pan.

2. Combine the flour, granulated sugar, brown sugar, baking powder, cinnamon, nutmeg, ginger, and cloves in a food processor and pulse to combine.

3. Add the butter pieces and pulse until combined and the mixture looks like coarse sand.

4. In a medium bowl, gently whisk the pumpkin, whipping cream, and egg until combined.

5. Transfer the dry ingredients to a large bowl and make a well in the center. Pour in the pumpkin mixture and gently combine with a rubber spatula. If the mixture does not come together easily, add ½ tablespoon more whipping cream.

6. Spoon 2-tablespoon portions of dough into each well of the prepared pan.

7. Bake until the tops are lightly browned, 15 to 20 minutes.

8. Allow to cool for 5 minutes in the pan, then carefully pop out with a thin plastic knife. Allow to cool completely on a cooling rack.

9. When the scookies are still slightly warm, use a spoon to place a healthy dollop of glaze on each one. Spread the glaze around with the back of the spoon. Sprinkle with granulated sugar, and allow the glaze to set for at least 1 hour.

10. Store in an airtight container for up to 2 days.

SWEET TIPS: *Buy pure canned pumpkin, not pumpkin pie filling.*

If you read the ingredients on "pumpkin pie spice" at the grocery store, you'll see that you probably already have the ingredients at home.

BLUEBERRY-LAVENDER SCOOKIES

Oh yeah, you can eat lavender.   VEGAN-FRIENDLY   MAKES 16

½ cup plus 1 tablespoon soy milk

1 teaspoon apple cider vinegar

1½ cups all-purpose flour

1 tablespoon baking powder

¼ teaspoon salt

¼ cup sugar

¼ cup vegan shortening, plus more for greasing the pan (we like Spectrum brand)

1 tablespoon canola oil

1 teaspoon vanilla extract

1½ cups blueberries, divided

2 tablespoons culinary lavender, chopped

1. Preheat the oven to 375°F. Grease a mini scone pan with vegan shortening.

2. Combine the soy milk and apple cider vinegar in a small bowl and set aside.

3. Sift the flour, baking powder, salt, and sugar into a large bowl. Add the shortening and combine with your fingers until the mixture looks like coarse sand.

4. Make a well in the center of the flour mixture and add the soy milk mixture, canola oil, and vanilla.

5. Gently combine with a rubber spatula, and when about halfway combined, toss in 1 cup of the blueberries and the lavender. Gently stir until completely combined.

6. Spoon 2-tablespoon portions of dough into each well of the prepared pan. Top the scookies with the remaining ½ cup blueberries.

7. Bake until the tops are golden and firm, 15 to 20 minutes.

8. Allow to cool for 5 minutes in the pan, then carefully pop out using a thin plastic knife. Allow to cool completely on a cooling rack.

9. Store at room temperature in an airtight container for up to 2 days.

SWEET TIPS: *Adding the blueberries and lavender when the milk is half combined prevents overmixing. If you add the blueberries too early, your scookies will turn purple.*

When placing the dough in the pan, be mindful of your blueberry distribution. It's ideal if there are not any blueberries on the bottom of your scookies, as they can stick to the pan and leave a void on the bottom of the scookie.

A knife is necessary to pop the scookies out of the pan, and a plastic one will prevent scratching the pan.

CHERRY-ALMOND-CARDAMOM SCOOKIES

Cardamom is magical. MAKES 16

1¾ cups all-purpose flour

2½ tablespoons baking powder

3 tablespoons sugar

¼ teaspoon salt

¼ teaspoon ground cardamom

6 tablespoons cold unsalted butter,
cut into ¼-inch cubes

½ tablespoon grated lemon zest

½ cup almond meal

¾ cup finely chopped dried cherries

1 large egg

¾ cup heavy whipping cream

1. Preheat the oven to 425°F. Spray a mini scone pan with cooking spray.

2. Combine the flour, baking powder, sugar, salt, and cardamom in a food processor and process to combine. With the processor running, add the butter one piece at a time and process until fully incorporated and the mixture looks like coarse sand. Add the lemon zest and pulse briefly. Add the almond meal and pulse briefly.

3. Transfer the mixture to a large bowl. Stir in the dried cherries.

4. In a small bowl, whisk together the egg and whipping cream.

5. Make a well in the center of the flour mixture and pour the egg mixture into it. Using a spatula, and then your hands, mix together to form a dough.

6. Using a 2-inch ice cream scoop, fill each well of the prepared pan. Shape the dough with your fingers to fit into each well.

7. Bake until golden and firm, about 20 minutes, rotating the pan halfway through.

8. Allow to cool for 5 minutes in the pan, then carefully pop out using a thin plastic knife. Allow to cool completely on a cooling rack.

9. Store at room temperature in an airtight container for up to 2 days.

SWEET TIPS: *You can make your own almond meal using a food processor and whole almonds. Just process until the almonds look like large crumbs.*

STRABERRY ROLLS

Like strawberry shortcake, in breakfast form. MAKES 24

FOR THE FILLING:

1 tablespoon cornstarch

1 tablespoon water

1 cup strawberries, coarsely chopped

¼ cup sugar

1 teaspoon vanilla extract

FOR THE DOUGH:

¾ teaspoon active dry yeast

¼ cup sugar

¼ teaspoon salt

1½ cups all-purpose flour, divided

¼ cup milk

2 tablespoons unsalted butter

¼ cup water

1 large egg, lightly beaten

FOR THE ICING:

½ teaspoon vanilla extract

1 tablespoon milk

½ cup powdered sugar, sifted

MAKE THE FILLING:

1. Mix the cornstarch and water until smooth. Set aside.

2. Combine the strawberries, sugar, and vanilla in a medium saucepan over medium-high heat for 1 to 2 minutes. When the sauce is liquid and combined, reduce the heat to low and whisk in the cornstarch mixture. Stir constantly for 3 minutes. Remove from the heat.

3. Set aside to cool completely.

MAKE THE DOUGH:

1. Sift together the yeast, sugar, salt, and ½ cup of the flour in a large bowl. Make a well in the center.

2. Heat the milk in a small saucepan over medium heat just until it boils. Remove from the heat. Add the butter and stir until combined. Add the water and allow the mixture to cool to just warm. If you're using a candy thermometer, the temperature should be between 100 and 110°F to properly activate the yeast.

3. Place the egg and the milk mixture in the well in the flour mixture. Stir well with a spatula until combined. Add the remaining the remaining 1 cup flour, ¼ cup at a time. Combine after each addition. If the flour isn't mixing in easily, add 1 to 2 tablespoons more water.

4. Transfer the dough to a lightly floured surface and knead for 8 minutes. The dough should be smooth and elastic.

FORM AND BAKE THE ROLLS:

1. Line a 9-inch square or round baking pan with parchment paper and spray the paper with cooking spray.

2. Roll the dough into a rectangle that is about 9 x 13 inches and ⅓ inch thick.

3. Spread the strawberry filling on the dough. Roll the dough into a log, starting with the long side. Use a little bit of water and your fingertips to seal the edge if needed. Place the log seam down, and slice into ½-inch rolls.

4. Place the rolls in the baking pan 1 inch apart. This will give them room to rise.

5. Cover loosely and allow to rise in a warm place for 1 hour.

6. Preheat the oven to 350°F.

7. Bake the rolls until golden brown, about 20 minutes.

8. Allow to cool for 20 minutes in the pan while you make the icing.

MAKE THE ICING:

1. Mix the vanilla and milk together in a small bowl.

2. In a medium bowl, gradually add the milk mixture to the powdered sugar and stir until combined. The icing should be a very thick liquid consistency.

3. Drizzle the icing on the cool rolls with a fork.

4. These are best the day they are made, but you can store them in an airtight container for up to 1 day.

SWEET TIPS: *For extra richness, you can spread 2 tablespoons of cream cheese on the dough along with the strawberry filling.*

HOT CROSS BUNS

These little delights are worth singing about. *MAKES 16*

FOR THE BUNS:

1¾ cups all-purpose flour, divided

½ teaspoon salt

¼ teaspoon ground cardamom

¼ teaspoon ground cinnamon

¼ teaspoon ground allspice

pinch of ground cloves

pinch of ground nutmeg

2 tablespoons plus ½ teaspoon sugar

¼ cup plus 2 tablespoons milk

1½ teaspoons active dry yeast

2 tablespoons unsalted butter, at room temperature

1 large egg, at room temperature

½ cup currants

⅓ cup candied citrus peel, finely chopped

1 teaspoon grated orange zest

1 large egg mixed with 1 tablespoon milk, for egg wash

FOR THE ICING:

¼ cup powdered sugar

1 teaspoon milk

MAKE THE BUNS:

1. Sift together 1½ cups of the flour and the salt, cardamom, cinnamon, allspice, cloves, nutmeg and 2 tablespoons of the sugar. Transfer the mixture to an electric mixer fitted with the paddle attachment and make a well in the center.

2. In a small saucepan over medium heat, warm the milk to 100 to 110°F. Monitor it with a candy thermometer. When the milk is warm, remove from the heat and pour ¼ cup into a medium bowl. Stir in the remaining

½ teaspoon sugar to the milk in the bowl. Sprinkle the yeast over the top and allow it to sit until foamy, about 5 minutes.

3. Pour the yeast mixture, the remaining warm milk, and the butter and eggs in the well in the dry ingredients. Beat on medium speed until all the ingredients are combined. The dough will be sticky.

4. With the mixer running, add the currants, candied citrus peel, and orange zest. Turn off the mixer and switch the attachment to the dough hook.

5. Knead on low for about 5 minutes until it has a doughy, elastic texture. With the mixer running, gradually sprinkle in the remaining ¼ cup flour until incorporated. Cover the bowl with plastic wrap and allow the dough to rise for 2 hours. It should double in size.

6. Line a rimmed baking sheet with parchment paper and spray the paper with cooking spray.

7. Punch down the dough while it's still in the bowl to release the air and condense it.

8. On a floured surface, flatten the dough into a log, and cut the log in half. Place one half back in the mixer bowl and re-cover it while you work with the other half.

9. Form the dough into 8 equal pieces by cutting it into 2 equal pieces and rolling them into 2 logs. Then cut each of those in half and roll them into logs again. Then cut the 4 logs in half.

10. Roll each piece of dough into a ball. Place on baking sheets ½ inch apart. Repeat with the remaining half of the dough.

11. Cover loosely and allow to rise in a warm place for 30 to 40 minutes. The buns should double in size.

12. Preheat the oven to 400°F.

13. Score the tops of the buns with a sharp knife. The cuts will need to be deep, as the buns will rise while baking.

14. Brush the egg wash onto the buns with a pastry brush.

15. Bake until lightly browned, 8 to 10 minutes. Allow to cool a few minutes on the pan, then transfer to a cooling rack to cool completely.

MAKE THE ICING:

1. Whisk together the powdered sugar and milk. It should be a thick consistency.

2. Transfer the icing to a plastic sandwich bag and trim off a corner.

3. When the buns are cool, pipe an X pattern over the top of each bun.

SWEET TIPS: *Candied citrus peel can be found at candy stores in the bulk bins.*

CRANBERRY ORANGE ROLLS

One tasty set of buns. MAKES 20

FOR THE ROLLS:

1½ cups all-purpose flour

½ teaspoon salt

1 packet (2¼ teaspoons) active dry yeast

3 tablespoons unsalted butter

1 large egg, gently beaten

½ cup milk

FOR THE FILLING:

¼ cup (½ stick) unsalted butter, at room temperature

¼ cup brown sugar, packed

1 tablespoon grated orange zest

2 teaspoons ground cinnamon

½ cup fresh cranberries, finely chopped

FOR THE GLAZE:

¾ cup powdered sugar

1 tablespoon orange juice

MAKE THE ROLLS:

1. Whisk together the flour, salt, and yeast in a large bowl. Using your hands, rub the butter into the flour until the mixture resembles coarse sand. Make a well in the center.

2. Gently whisk the egg in a small bowl and set aside.

3. Heat the milk to 100 to 110°F in a medium saucepan over medium heat. Monitor it with a candy thermometer.

4. Pour the egg and heated milk into the well in the flour. Working quickly so the egg doesn't start to cook, bring the dough together with your hands to form a ball.

5. Cover and set aside to rise in a warm place until doubled in size, about 40 minutes.

MAKE THE FILLING:

1. Combine the butter, brown sugar, orange zest, and cinnamon in an electric mixer fitted with the paddle attachment. Beat on medium speed until combined and fluffy, about 2 minutes.

ASSEMBLE:

1. Spray a 9-inch round cake pan with cooking spray.

2. Punch the dough to deflate, about 30 seconds.

3. On a generously floured surface, roll the dough into a rectangle that is about 12 x 9 inches and ¼ inch thick. Cut the dough in half lengthwise with a pizza cutter.

4. Spread the filling on the 2 strips of dough, avoiding the very edges. Sprinkle the cranberries on top.

5. Roll each piece of dough lengthwise to form 2 long strips. Trim off the uneven ends. Cut each roll into 1-inch segments, reforming each segment into a bitty bun as needed. Place in the prepared pan about ¼ inch apart. Cover and let rise for 30 minutes. Reform into bitty buns as needed before baking, as they can lose their shape during the last rise.

6. Preheat the oven to 375°F. Bake until risen and lightly golden, about 20 minutes.

7. Allow to cool for 5 minutes while you make the glaze.

MAKE THE GLAZE:

1. Combine the powdered sugar and orange juice in a small bowl. Drizzle over the bitty buns in the pan and allow to set.

2. Store in an airtight container for up to 2 days.

SWEET TIPS: *If your kitchen is chilly, preheat the oven and allow the rolls to rise on top of the oven, or let them rise in the oven with the light on.*

FRESH LEMON ZEST COFFEE CAKE

A zesty way to start your day.   MAKES 12

FOR THE CAKE:

1 cup all-purpose flour

½ teaspoon baking powder

1 teaspoon baking soda

1 teaspoon salt

¼ cup (½ stick) unsalted butter, at room temperature

½ cup sugar

1 tablespoon grated lemon zest

1 large egg

1 teaspoon vanilla extract

1 teaspoon lemon extract

½ cup sour cream

1 recipe Classic Streusel (page 134) made with ½ teaspoon lemon extract

FOR THE GLAZE:

1 teaspoon grated lemon zest

2 tablespoons lemon juice

½ cup powdered sugar

MAKE THE CAKE:

1. Preheat the oven to 350°F. Line a standard 12-well muffin pan with paper liners, or spray with cooking spray if you have a quality pan.

2. Sift together the flour, baking powder, baking soda, and salt in a medium bowl.

3. Combine the butter, sugar, and lemon zest in an electric mixer fitted with the paddle attachment. Beat until pale and fluffy, about 3 minutes. Reduce the mixer speed to low. Add the egg, vanilla extract, and lemon extract,

scraping down the bowl as needed. Add half the flour mixture, then half the sour cream, mixing to combine thoroughly after each addition. Next add the remaining flour mixture, then the remaining sour cream.

4. Using a 2-inch ice cream scoop that is a little over halfway full, scoop the batter into each well in the muffin pan. The cakes will rise quite a bit, so do not worry if the level looks low. Sprinkle each cake with a very generous portion of the streusel. It's OK if it looks messy and if some of the streusel falls into the sides of the muffins.

5. Bake until risen and firm to the touch and a toothpick inserted into the center returns with no crumbs, about 30 minutes, rotating the pan halfway through. Allow to cool 5 minutes in the pan, then remove as soon as safely possible. Allow to cool completely on cooling racks.

SWEET TIPS: *For the best zest, get firm organic lemons.*

You need about 3 lemons for this recipe.

MAKE THE GLAZE:

1. Combine all the ingredients in a small bowl. Stir to combine with a spatula. Drizzle over the completely cooled coffee cakes.

2. Coffee cakes are best when eaten on the same day they are baked. However, you can store them in an airtight container for up to 2 days.

HAZELNUT AND FIG COFFEE CAKE

It fig-ures. MAKES 12

FOR THE STREUSEL:

½ cup hazelnut meal

3 tablespoons cold unsalted butter, diced

¼ cup brown sugar, packed

FOR THE CAKE:

I cup all-purpose flour

½ teaspoon baking powder

I teaspoon baking soda

I teaspoon salt

½ cup hazelnut meal

¼ cup (½ stick) unsalted butter, at room temperature

½ cup sugar

2 large eggs

I teaspoon vanilla extract

¾ cup sour cream

¼ cup finely chopped dried figs

MAKE THE STREUSEL:

1. Combine all the ingredients in a large bowl and blend with your fingers until the mixture looks like coarse sand. Cover and refrigerate.

MAKE THE CAKE:

1. Preheat the oven to 350°F. Line 12 standard muffin wells with paper liners, or spray with cooking spray if you have a quality pan.

2. Sift together the flour, baking powder, baking soda, and salt in a medium bowl. Stir in the hazelnut meal by hand.

3. Combine the butter and sugar in an electric mixer fitted with the paddle attachment. Beat on medium speed until pale and fluffy, about 3 minutes. Reduce the mixer speed to low. Add the eggs and vanilla extract, scraping down the bowl as needed. Add half the flour mixture, then half the sour cream, mixing to combine thoroughly after each addition. Next add the remaining flour mixture, then the remaining sour cream. Add the figs and mix until just combined.

4. Using a 2-inch ice cream scoop a little more than halfway full, scoop the batter into each well of the muffin pan. The cakes will rise quite a bit, so don't worry if the level looks low. Sprinkle each cake with a very generous portion of the streusel. Remove any stray streusel from the top of the pan.

5. Bake for 30 minutes, rotating the pan once halfway through. Allow to cool 5 minutes in the pan, or until safe to handle, then transfer to a cooling rack to cool completely.

6. Coffee cakes are best when eaten on the same day they are baked. However, you can store them in an airtight container for up to 2 days.

SWEET TIPS: *You may need to knock the excess streusel off the edges of the cakes after baking.*

If your store doesn't carry hazelnut meal (we use Bob's Red Mill brand), you can purchase whole hazelnuts and grind them to a meal in your food processor.

CRANBERRY-VANILLA COFFEE CAKE

Get your morning off to a delicious start.   MAKES 12

½ vanilla bean, split lengthwise

1¾ cup sugar

1 cup fresh cranberries

2 cups plus 1 tablespoon all-purpose flour, divided

2 teaspoons baking powder

¾ teaspoon salt

¼ cup plus 1 tablespoon unsalted butter, at room temperature, divided

2 large eggs

½ cup heavy whipping cream

powdered sugar, for dusting

1. Preheat the oven to 375°F. Line a standard 12-well muffin pan with paper liners.

2. Scrape the vanilla bean into a food processor fitted with a blade. Discard the pod.

3. Add the sugar and pulse until combined. Transfer all but ¼ cup to a medium bowl.

4. Add the cranberries to the food processor. Pulse briefly until the cranberries are coarsely chopped but not pureed.

5. In a medium bowl, sift together 2 cups of the flour and the baking powder and salt.

6. In an electric mixer fitted with the paddle attachment, combine ¼ cup of the butter and ½ cup of the vanilla-sugar mixture. Beat on medium until pale and fluffy.

SWEET TIPS: *Using the pure vanilla bean may seem like extra work, but it's worth it. And you'll look like a total pro.*

7. Beat in the eggs one at a time, mixing fully after each one and scraping down the bowl as needed.

8. Reduce the speed to low. Add half the flour mixture, then half the whipping cream, then the remaining flour, then the remaining whipping cream, scraping down the bowl as needed.

9. Using a 2-inch ice cream scoop, fill each muffin liner halfway full. Place a dollop of cranberry sugar on top of the batter, avoiding the edges. Top with the remaining batter, filling each liner three-quarters full.

10. Add the remaining 1 tablespoon butter and 1 tablespoon flour to the remaining vanilla sugar. Blend with your hands until combined. Sprinkle over the top of each cake.

11. Bake until a toothpick inserted into the center returns with no crumbs. The toothpick may return with cranberries on it, and that's OK.

12. Allow to cool for 15 minutes in the pan, then transfer to a cooling rack to cool completely. Use a fine-mesh sieve to dust with powdered sugar before serving.

13. Store in an airtight container for up to 2 days.

SWEET
SNACKS

Ahhh...guilty pleasures. These scrumptious little bites are the ones we eat in the middle of the afternoon when we aren't even hungry. You don't need a reason or a special occasion to whip up a batch of mini cupcakes, brownie bites, or sprinkled mini donuts. If you make a whole batch and don't even share, we won't tell.

ESPRESSO BROWNIES

Another salute to our beloved Emerald City.   MAKES 24

FOR THE BROWNIES:

3 ounces semisweet chocolate
  baking squares

¼ cup (½ stick) plus 2 tablespoons
  unsalted butter

2 tablespoons unsweetened cocoa powder

¾ cup all-purpose flour

¼ teaspoon baking powder

¼ teaspoon salt

2 large eggs

1 cup sugar

2 teaspoons vanilla extract

2 tablespoons espresso powder

¾ cup semisweet mini chocolate chips

FOR THE ICING:

2 teaspoons espresso powder

2 tablespoons water

2 tablespoons unsalted butter,
  at room temperature

1½ cups powdered sugar

1 teaspoon vanilla extract

MAKE THE BROWNIES:

1. Preheat the oven to 350°F. Line a 9 x 9-inch pan with waxed paper, and coat the waxed paper with cooking spray.

2. Combine the chocolate, butter, and cocoa powder in a medium saucepan over low heat. Melt and stir to combine. Remove from the heat and allow to cool for 5 minutes.

3. Sift the flour, baking powder, and salt together in a medium bowl.

4. In an electric mixer fitted with the whisk attachment, beat the eggs, sugar, and vanilla for 4 minutes on medium speed. The mixture should look pale when finished.

5. Reduce the speed to low. Add the espresso powder, the chocolate mixture, and the flour mixture, beating well after each addition before adding the next. Beat until combined, scraping down the bowl as needed.

6. Mix in the mini chocolate chips by hand.

7. Pour the batter into the prepared pan. Bake for 35 minutes, rotating the pan once halfway through. Allow to cool completely in the pan.

MAKE THE ICING:

1. Dissolve the espresso in the water. When dissolved, place in the bowl of an electric mixer fitted with the whisk attachment. Add the butter, powdered sugar, and vanilla and beat until completely combined, about 2 minutes.

2. When the brownies have cooled, pour the icing on top and spread with a spatula to coat evenly. Cover and refrigerate overnight. Use the waxed paper to transfer the brownies from the pan to a cutting board. Slice into 1½-inch squares, being careful that the waxed paper doesn't stick to the brownies, and serve.

SWEET TIPS: *If you sample these brownies in the evening, you'll be up all night. They are potent. You've been warned.*

We normally ignore directions to stir ingredients in by hand and use the electric mixer instead. But hand mixing is important here, as the mini chocolate chips will get caught in your whisk.

F.U. BROWNIES

Reviews of these are so good they're laced with profanity.   MAKES 18

⅔ cup all-purpose flour

¼ cup unsweetened cocoa powder

1½ teaspoons ground ginger

½ teaspoon ground nutmeg

⅛ teaspoon ground cloves

½ teaspoon salt

2 large eggs

½ teaspoon vanilla extract

3 ounces semisweet chocolate baking squares

½ cup (1 stick) unsalted butter

1 cup sugar

1. Preheat the oven to 325°F. Heavily butter 18 mini muffin wells.

2. Sift together the flour, cocoa powder, ginger, nutmeg, cloves, and salt in a large bowl.

3. Whisk the eggs and vanilla together in a small bowl.

4. In a medium saucepan over low heat, gently melt the chocolate and butter together. Remove from the heat as soon as combined. Stir in the egg mixture, then stir in the dry ingredients.

5. Using a 1-inch ice cream scoop and heaping scoops, fill the prepared muffin wells. Bake for 25 minutes, rotating the pan once halfway through.

6. Allow to cool 5 minutes in the pan, then turn out onto a cooling rack to cool completely. Store in an airtight container for up to 2 days.

MRS. RANDALL'S BROWNIES

Gluten-free and sugar-free, but luckily not taste-free.   MAKES 20

1 teaspoon Stevia powder, or
   other all-natural sweetener

2 teaspoons boiling water

¼ cup plus 2 tablespoons vegetable oil

2 large eggs

½ cup agave nectar

¾ cup hazelnut meal

½ cup unsweetened cocoa powder

¼ cup arrowroot flour

1. Preheat the oven to 350°F. Spray 20 mini muffin wells with cooking spray.

2. Place the Stevia in a medium heatproof bowl. Pour the boiling water over the Stevia and stir to combine.

3. Add the oil, eggs, and agave nectar to the Stevia and stir to combine.

4. In a large bowl, mix together the hazelnut meal, cocoa powder, and arrowroot flour.

5. Make a well in the center of the dry mixture and pour the wet mixture into it. Stir with a spatula until combined.

6. Using a 1-inch ice cream scoop and level scoops, fill each prepared muffin well with the batter.

7. Bake until a toothpick inserted into the center returns with no crumbs, about 25 minutes, rotating the pan once halfway through.

8. Allow to cool for 5 minutes in the pan, or until safe to handle. Then transfer to a cooling rack to cool completely.

9. Store in an airtight container for up to 3 days.

> **SWEET TIPS:** *The hazelnut meal is key to this recipe. If you are unable to find hazelnut meal, you can purchase whole hazelnuts and grind them yourself in a coffee grinder or food processor.*

CHOCOLATE STOUT CUPCAKES WITH IRISH CREAM FROSTING

The luck o' the Irish, wrapped into one little cupcake. MAKES 24

FOR THE CUPCAKES:

½ cup soy milk

1 teaspoon apple cider vinegar

1 cup plus 2 tablespoons all-purpose flour

⅓ cup unsweetened Dutch process cocoa powder

½ teaspoon baking soda

½ teaspoon baking powder

¼ teaspoon salt

¾ cup sugar

½ cup chocolate stout (we like Young's Double Chocolate)

⅓ cup canola oil

1½ teaspoons vanilla extract

FOR THE FROSTING:

½ cup (1 stick) unsalted butter, at room temperature

3 cups powdered sugar, sifted

¼ cup Baileys Irish Cream liqueur

1 to 2 tablespoons soy milk

¼ cup mini chocolate chips, for topping

MAKE THE CUPCAKES:

1. Preheat the oven to 350°F and line 24 mini muffin wells with paper liners.

2. Combine the soy milk and vinegar in the bowl of a stand mixer and set aside to curdle for a few minutes.

3. Sift together the flour, cocoa, baking soda, baking powder, salt, and sugar in a medium bowl. Set aside.

4. Add the stout, oil, and vanilla to the mixer bowl fitted with the paddle attachment. Beat on medium speed until frothy.

5. With the mixer running, gradually add the flour mixture and beat until fully combined, about 2 minutes.

6. Using a 1-inch ice cream scoop, fill each cupcake liner to just below the brim.

7. Bake until the tops spring back when touched and a toothpick inserted into the center returns with no crumbs, 20 to 22 minutes.

8. Allow to cool for 5 minutes in the pan, then transfer to cooling racks to cool completely.

MAKE THE FROSTING:

1. In an electric mixer fitted with the paddle attachment, beat the butter on medium speed until fluffy.

2. Add the powdered sugar ½ cup at a time, incorporating after each addition.

3. Add the Baileys and whip on medium speed for 5 minutes. If the mixture is too dry, add 1 to 2 tablespoons soy milk.

4. Transfer the frosting into a pastry bag fitted with a plain tip and frost each cupcake generously. Top each cupcake with a few mini chocolate chips.

5. Store in an airtight container for up to 2 days.

SWEET TIPS: *For vegan-friendly frosting, use a vegan buttery stick in place of the butter. Keep in mind that Baileys isn't vegan, so make sure your friends are OK with that. If they are sticklers, you can substitute Very Best Buttercream (page 132) for the Baileys frosting.*

WHISKEY MAPLE BACON MINI CUPCAKES

An entire breakfast delivered to you in one bite.   MAKES 2 DOZEN

FOR THE CUPCAKES:

4 strips bacon

½ teaspoon apple cider vinegar

½ cup soy milk

1⅓ cups all-purpose flour

¾ teaspoon baking powder

½ teaspoon baking soda

½ teaspoon salt

⅛ teaspoon ground nutmeg

½ cup pure maple syrup

2 tablespoons brown sugar

½ teaspoon vanilla extract

FOR THE FROSTING:

¼ cup (½ stick) unsalted butter

¼ cup shortening

2 cups powdered sugar, sifted

¼ cup soy milk

1 tablespoon whiskey

2 teaspoons pure maple syrup

bacon bits (cooked during cupcake making)

MAKE THE CUPCAKES:

1. Preheat the oven to 350°F and line 24 mini muffin wells with paper liners.

2. Cook the bacon in a frying pan until crispy curls form, making sure not to burn it. Save ⅓ cup of the drippings. Cool and drain the bacon on a paper towel. Crumble and reserve it for topping the cupcakes.

3. Combine the apple cider vinegar with the soy milk in a small bowl and set aside.

4. Sift together the flour, baking powder, baking soda, salt, and nutmeg in a large bowl.

5. In a stand mixer fitted with the paddle attachment, combine the soy milk mixture, maple syrup, bacon drippings, brown sugar, and vanilla on medium speed.

6. Reduce the speed to medium-low and, with the mixer running, gradually add the flour mixture and mix until no lumps remain.

7. Using a mini ice cream scoop, scoop the batter into the liners, filling each to just below the brim. Bake until the tops are a light golden brown, 18 to 20 minutes.

8. Allow to cool for 5 minutes in the pan, then transfer to a cooling rack to cool completely.

MAKE THE FROSTING

1. In a stand mixer fitted with the paddle attachment, beat together the butter and shortening on medium speed until fluffy.

2. Add the powdered sugar and whip on medium speed for 3 minutes. Add the soy milk, whiskey, and maple syrup and whip until creamy, 5 to 7 minutes, adding more soy milk if needed.

3. Using a pastry bag or cupcake froster, frost the cooled cupcakes. Top with the bacon bits.

4. Store at room temperature in an airtight container for up to 2 days.

SWEET TIPS: *The bacon for this recipe should be as plain as possible. Avoid anything hickory smoked or flavored; thick-cut isn't necessary. Cook the bacon with butter for added flavor. If there aren't enough drippings, either cook more bacon or top off with canola oil.*

Make sure you use good-quality maple syrup; it really does matter.

FAUXSTESS CUPCAKES

One tasty little imposter. MAKES 24

FOR THE CUPCAKES:

I cup all-purpose flour

⅓ cup unsweetened cocoa powder

¾ teaspoon baking soda

¼ teaspoon salt

⅓ cup canola oil

⅔ cup sugar

¼ cup unsweetened applesauce

½ teaspoon vanilla extract

⅓ cup water

⅓ cup milk

FOR THE WHITE FILLING:

3 tablespoons unsalted butter,
    at room temperature

¼ cup plus I tablespoon
    powdered sugar, sifted

½ teaspoon vanilla extract

⅛ teaspoon salt

generous½ cup marshmallow fluff

FOR THE CHOCOLATE FROSTING:

2 tablespoons unsalted butter,
    at room temperature

½ cup semisweet chocolate chips

I tablespoon pure maple syrup

¼ teaspoon vanilla extract

MAKE THE CUPCAKES:

I. Preheat the oven to 375°F. Line 24 mini muffin wells with paper liners.

2. In a medium bowl, sift together the flour, cocoa powder, baking soda, and salt.

3. In an electric mixer, beat the oil and sugar on medium-low until combined. Reduce the speed to low. Add the applesauce and mix until combined. Add the vanilla and mix until combined.

4. Add half the flour mixture and half the water, then the remaining flour mixture and the remaining water, allowing each to fully incorporate before adding the next. Scrape down the bowl as needed.

5. With the mixer running, gradually pour in the milk in a steady stream and mix until combined. Scrape down the bowl as needed.

6. Using a 1-inch ice cream scoop, fill each cupcake liner to just below the brim. You want the cupcakes to puff up over the top of the liner as they bake so they are easier to frost. You'll see.

7. Bake until a toothpick inserted into the center returns with only a few crumbs, 15 to 18 minutes, rotating the pan halfway through.

8. Allow to cool for 5 minutes in the pan, then transfer to a cooling rack to cool completely.

MAKE THE WHITE FILLING:

1. In an electric mixer fitted with the paddle attachment, mix the butter and sugar until creamy but not fluffy, about 3 minutes. With the mixer running, add the vanilla and salt. Add the marshmallow fluff and mix until combined and fluffy.

2. Transfer the filling to a medium bowl. Cover with plastic wrap and refrigerate to thicken for 30 minutes.

MAKE THE CHOCOLATE FROSTING:

1. In a small saucepan, combine the butter, chocolate chips, and maple syrup over very low heat. Stirring constantly, melt the ingredients together until combined and shiny. Remove from the heat and add the vanilla.

2. Transfer to a medium bowl. Cover with plastic wrap and refrigerate to thicken for 20 minutes.

FILL AND DECORATE:

1. Remove the cold white filling and chocolate frosting from the fridge. Transfer the white filling into a pastry bag with a long filler tip; the smaller the end of the tip, the better.

2. Stick the filler tip into the center of each cupcake halfway from the top; be careful not to insert the tip too far. Gently (but firmly) squeeze the bag to fill. When you feel resistance, the cupcake is "full." You should have filling left over for the white swirl design on top of each cupcake.

3. Turn each cupcake upside down into the chocolate frosting bowl and coat the tops in the chocolate frosting.

4. Refrigerate the cupcakes for 20 minutes to set the frosting. Refrigerate the white filling in the pastry bag, too.

5. Using the remainder of the white filling, decorate each cupcake with the traditional swirl design across the equator.

6. Refrigerate the completed cupcakes for a final 30 minutes to set all the frosting. Serve the same day.

GREEN TEA-POMEGRANATE CUPCAKES

So fancy. So hip. So delicious.   MAKES 24

FOR THE CUPCAKES:

1¼ cups all-purpose flour

¾ cup sugar

1 teaspoon baking powder

¼ teaspoon baking soda

1 tablespoon matcha tea powder

¼ teaspoon salt

½ cup plain soy yogurt

⅔ cup rice milk

¼ teaspoon vanilla

½ teaspoon almond extract

⅓ cup canola oil

¼ cup pomegranate seeds

FOR THE POMEGRANATE FOAM:

½ cup pomegranate juice

1 tablespoon sugar

3 large egg whites

MAKE THE CUPCAKES:

1. Preheat the oven to 350°F. Line 24 mini muffin wells with paper liners.

2. In a medium bowl, sift together the flour, sugar, baking powder, baking soda, matcha, and salt.

3. In an electric mixer fitted with the whisk attachment, beat the yogurt, rice milk, vanilla, almond extract, and oil until combined, about 2 minutes.

4. With the mixer running, gradually add the flour mixture. Fold in the pomegranate seeds by hand.

5. Fill each cupcake liner three-quarters full. Bake until firm to the touch and a toothpick inserted into the center returns with no crumbs, about 20 minutes, rotating the pan halfway through.

6. Allow to cool in the pan for 5 minutes, then transfer to a cooling rack to cool completely.

MAKE THE POMEGRANATE FOAM:

1. Combine the pomegranate juice and sugar in a medium saucepan over medium heat until boiling. Reduce the heat to medium-low and simmer until the mixture has reduced in volume and thickened, 6 to 8 minutes. Reduce the heat to low.

2. In an electric mixer fitted with the whisk attachment, beat the egg whites on medium speed until foamy, about 3 minutes.

3. With the mixer running on medium speed, gradually pour the hot pomegranate juice into the egg whites in a steady stream. Continue beating until the mixture has cooled, about 8 minutes.

4. Turn off the mixer. Using a teaspoon, place a healthy dollop of pomegranate foam on top of each completely cooled cupcake.

5. Refrigerate in an airtight container for up to 2 days.

PISTACHIO-ROSEWATER YIPPIE PIES

Pure magic. And pistachios.   VEGAN-FRIENDLY   MAKES 12

1 cup plus 2 tablespoons all-purpose flour

2 tablespoons cornstarch

½ teaspoon baking soda

½ teaspoon baking powder

generous pinch of ground cardamom

¼ teaspoon salt

½ cup vanilla soy yogurt

⅔ cup soy milk

⅓ cup canola oil

½ cup plus 2 tablespoons sugar

2 tablespoons rosewater

⅔ cup chopped pistachios, divided

Very Best Buttercream (page 132) made with 1 tablespoon rose water added to the soy milk

1. Preheat the oven to 350°F. Spray a mini whoopie pie pan with cooking spray.

2. Sift the flour, cornstarch, baking soda, baking powder, cardamom, and salt together in a medium bowl. Set aside.

3. In a large bowl, whisk together the yogurt, soy milk, oil, sugar, and rosewater.

4. Gradually add the flour mixture to the wet ingredients. Mix with a spatula until combined and no lumps remain. Mix in ⅓ cup of the pistachios.

5. Using a 1-inch ice cream scoop, fill each well in the prepared pan to just below the brim, working in batches if needed to get 24 total pie halves. Bake until lightly browned and the tops spring back when touched, about 22 minutes, rotating the pan halfway through.

SWEET TIP: *Be sure to buy culinary rosewater for this recipe.*

6. Allow to cool for 2 minutes in the pan, then transfer to a cooling rack to cool completely.

7. Transfer the frosting into a pastry bag fitted with a medium tip. Rose tips are nice for details at the edges, but not necessary.

8. Sort the pie pieces according to size and pair up accordingly. Pipe frosting on one side of each pie and top with the second piece.

9. Place the remaining ⅓ cup pistachios on a plate. Roll the sides of each whoopie pie in the pistachios so that the nuts stick to the frosting around the edges.

10. Store in an airtight container for up to 2 days.

RED VELVET YIPPIE PIES

"...in that little boy's smile."   MAKES 15

1¼ cups all-purpose flour

1 cup sugar

3 tablespoons unsweetened cocoa powder

1 teaspoon baking powder

¼ teaspoon salt

8 ounces canned beets in juice

⅓ cup canola oil

2 tablespoons lemon juice

1 teaspoon vanilla extract

1 recipe Very Best Buttercream (page 132)

1. Preheat the oven to 350°F. Spray a mini whoopie pie pan with cooking spray.

2. Sift together the flour, sugar, cocoa powder, baking powder, and salt in a medium bowl.

3. Puree the beets and their juice in a food processor until combined.

4. Stir together the beet puree, oil, lemon juice, and vanilla in a large bowl.

5. Gradually stir the flour mixture into the beet mixture.

6. Using a 1-inch ice cream scoop, fill each well in the prepared pan to the brim, working in batches if needed to get 30 total pie halves. Bake until the tops spring back when touched, 18 to 20 minutes, rotating the pan halfway through.

7. Allow to cool for 2 minutes in the pan, then transfer to a cooling rack to cool completely.

8. Transfer the buttercream into a pastry bag fitted with a medium tip. Rose tips are nice for details at the edges, but not necessary.

9. Sort the pie pieces according to size and pair up accordingly. Pipe frosting on one side of each pie and top with a second piece.

10. Store in an airtight container for up to 2 days.

BUNNY RABBIT CARROT CAKE WHOOPIE PIES

Making Peter Cottontail proud.   MAKES 8

FOR THE CAKES:

¾ cup all-purpose flour

1 teaspoon baking soda

¼ teaspoon salt

1 teaspoon ground cinnamon

½ teaspoon ground nutmeg

1 large egg

⅓ cup vegetable oil

½ cup brown sugar, packed

1 teaspoon vanilla extract

1 cup shredded carrot (about 2 carrots)

¼ cup peeled and grated apple
   (we like Granny Smith)

¼ cup unsweetened flaked coconut

¼ cup finely chopped walnuts
   (chopped in a food processor)

FOR THE FROSTING:

¼ cup (½ stick) unsalted butter,
   at room temperature

4 ounces cream cheese, at
   room temperature

1 tablespoon pure molasses

½ cup plus 3 tablespoons powdered sugar

a few drops orange food coloring (optional)

MAKE THE CAKES:

1. Preheat the oven to 350°F. Spray a bunny rabbit–shaped mini whoopie pie pan with cooking spray.

2. Sift together the flour, baking soda, salt, cinnamon, and nutmeg in a medium bowl.

3. In an electric mixer fitted with the paddle attachment, lightly beat the egg on low speed. Add the oil, brown sugar, and vanilla. Beat until combined. Gradually add the flour mixture and mix until combined. Mix in the carrot, apple, coconut, and walnuts.

4. Using a 1-inch ice cream scoop and almost full scoops, fill each well of the prepared pan with batter, working in batches if needed to get 16 pie halves total. Bake until lightly browned and firm to the touch, about 15 minutes, rotating the pan halfway through. Allow to cool for 5 minutes in the pan, then transfer to a cutting board to finish cooling.

MAKE THE FROSTING:

1. In the bowl of an electric mixer, beat the butter and cream cheese on medium speed until combined. Mix in the molasses. Gradually add the powdered sugar and mix until combined. Add a few drops of orange food coloring, if using, and mix until combined.

2. Load the frosting into a pastry bag fitted with a fine tip and refrigerate for 30 minutes.

ASSEMBLE THE PIES:

1. Examine the whoopie pies and if they have rounded bottoms, carefully use a serrated knife to trim the rounded part.

2. Pipe a generous amount of cold frosting on a bunny rabbit, and top with a second bunny rabbit. With the fine tip of the pastry bag, you can add an eye and a fluffy tail to the top bunny.

3. Refrigerate in an airtight container for up to 2 days.

SWEET TIPS: *There will be leftover cake when you trim the cakes to be flat. Eat it.*

If you use a traditional round mini whoopie pie pan, the recipe will make more than 8.

BOSTON CREAM YIPPIE PIES

For Ashley, who is wicked awesome.   MAKES 20

FOR THE CUSTARD FILLING:
I cup whole milk
¼ cup sugar, divided
2 large egg yolks
I teaspoon vanilla extract
½ teaspoon ground cinnamon
⅛ teaspoon salt
3 tablespoons cornstarch

FOR THE CAKES:
⅔ cup fine cake flour
⅔ teaspoon baking powder
⅓ teaspoon salt
I whole large egg plus I egg yolk
⅔ cup sugar
I tablespoon unsalted butter
⅓ cup plus I tablespoon whole milk
I teaspoon vanilla extract

FOR THE CHOCOLATE GLAZE:
4 ounces semisweet chocolate
  baking squares
½ cup heavy whipping cream

MAKE THE CUSTARD FILLING ONE DAY AHEAD:

1. Heat the milk and ⅛ cup of the sugar in a medium saucepan over low heat. Bring to a simmer; do not allow to boil.

2. Meanwhile, in an electric mixer fitted with the whisk attachment, whisk the eggs yolks and remaining ⅛ cup sugar on medium speed until combined, about

1 minute. With the mixer running, add the vanilla, cinnamon, and salt. Next, gradually add the cornstarch 1 tablespoon at a time. Reduce the speed to low.

3. Remove the milk mixture from the heat. Slowly pour half of the hot milk mixture into the mixer bowl in a steady stream. Mix until just combined.

4. Pour the egg mixture from the mixer bowl into the saucepan. Turn the heat to medium and whisk constantly for 5 minutes, bringing the custard to a wicked hot boil.

5. Pour the custard into a heatproof bowl. Cover with plastic wrap, pressing the plastic against the top of the custard. This will prevent a film from forming on top.

6. Refrigerate overnight so it sets like the ice on the Common in January.

MAKE THE CAKES:

1. Preheat the oven to 350°F. Spray a mini whoopie pie pan with cooking spray.

2. Sift together the flour, baking powder, and salt.

3. Place the whole egg and egg yolk in an electric mixer fitted with the whisk attachment. Whisk on medium speed for 1 minute. With the mixer running, gradually sprinkle in the sugar and continue beating for 3 more minutes.

4. Meanwhile, combine the butter and milk in a small saucepan over medium heat until melted. Do not bring to a boil. Remove from the heat and stir in the vanilla.

5. With the mixer still on medium speed, gradually pour the hot milk mixture into the egg mixture in a steady stream. After the milk is combined, gradually add the flour mixture and mix until combined.

6. Using a 1-inch ice cream scoop that is three-quarters full, spoon the batter into the prepared pan. Bake until puffed up out of the pan and the edges are browned, about 12 minutes, rotating the pan halfway through. The tops will still look spongy. Remove from the pan as soon as safely possible and transfer to cooling racks to cool completely.

7. Re-load the pan with the remaining batter and bake. Allow all the cakes to cool completely.

FILL THE CAKES:

1. Place the cold custard filling in an electric mixer fitted with the whisk attachment. Whisk for 3 minutes until it loosens up and resembles custard again. If you have a splash guard for your mixer, you'll want to use it, 'cause it gets wicked messy.

2. Transfer the custard filling into a pastry bag fitted with a flower tip.

3. Assemble the whoopie pies. Pipe a healthy dollop of the filling onto the spongy side of half of the cakes. Top each one with the remaining cakes, leaving the browned side on the outside.

MAKE THE GLAZE AFTER THE CAKES ARE COOLED AND FILLED:

1. Chop the chocolate into small pieces and place in a heatproof bowl.

2. Heat the heavy cream in a small saucepan and bring to a boil over medium heat. Pour the hot milk over the chocolate and stir with a spatula until combined. Allow to cool for 5 minutes.

3. Using a spoon, coat the top of each yippie pie with a thick layer of the chocolate. Encourage the chocolate to spread down the sides by swirling the back of the spoon on top of the pie. Add more chocolate as necessary. Allow the chocolate to cool and firm up a bit.

4. Refrigerate in an airtight container for up to 2 days.

SWEET TIPS: *Purists or people from Boston will want to leave the cinnamon out of the filling. That's OK.*

The filling will look like a strange blob when you remove it from the fridge. Have faith and turn on the mixer. It'll look like filling again within a few minutes.

Bring your whisking A-game and don't stop whisking—the custard mixture thickens rapidly!

You can use a heart-shaped mini whoopie pie pan for these, too. In this case, the recipe makes about 10 pies.

JELLY DONUTS

Even Santa would be jealous.   MAKES 12

FOR THE DONUTS:

1 teaspoon honey

1 packet (2¼ tablespoons)
   active dry yeast

½ cup warm water (110 to 125°F)

1½ cups bread flour

¾ cup sugar, divided

3 teaspoons ground cinnamon, divided

1 teaspoon salt

½ teaspoon ground nutmeg

1 large egg

vegetable oil, for frying

FOR THE JELLY:

1½ cups fresh raspberries

1½ cups fresh blackberries

¾ cup sugar

1½ tablespoons lemon juice

1½ tablespoons cornstarch

MAKE THE DONUTS:

1. Place the honey and yeast in a small bowl. Pour in the warm water and stir very gently. Set aside for 5 minutes to rise and foam. If the yeast does not foam, start over with different yeast.

2. In a medium bowl, stir together the flour, ¼ cup of the sugar, 1 teaspoon of the cinnamon, and the salt and nutmeg.

3. Butter the bowl of an electric mixer or spray with cooking spray. Attach the dough hook to the mixer. Place the egg in the mixer bowl and turn the speed to low. Add the yeast mixture. Gradually add the flour mixture, scraping down

the bowl as needed. When combined, knead with the mixer on low for 5 minutes.

4. Cover with a towel and allow to rise in a warm, dry place until doubled, about 1½ hours. While the dough rises, you can make the jelly (see below).

5. Line a rimmed baking sheet with waxed paper and spray the paper with cooking spray.

6. On a thoroughly floured surface, roll out the dough to ½-inch thick. Using a 1½-inch-diameter cookie cutter, cut out donuts and place on the prepared baking sheet. Re-roll the dough as needed. Reserve any tiny dough bits left over for testing the oil. Cover the donuts with a light cloth and allow to rise for 20 more minutes.

7. Meanwhile, combine the remaining ½ cup sugar and 2 teaspoons cinnamon in a small bowl.

8. In a small skillet over medium-high heat, heat 1 inch of vegetable oil. Test the oil for readiness by dropping tiny bits of dough into the oil. If the bits begin to fry, the oil is ready.

9. Very carefully, using metal tongs, place 3 to 4 donuts in the skillet and fry for 30 seconds on each side. Use the tongs to remove the donuts from the oil and roll each warm donut in the cinnamon sugar and place on a paper towel to cool.

MAKE THE JELLY:

1. Combine the raspberries, blackberries, sugar, and lemon juice in a small saucepan. Simmer over low heat for 10 minutes. Mash the berries with a potato

masher or spatula. Simmer for 10 more minutes. Remove from the heat and stir in the cornstarch. Allow to cool.

FILL THE DONUTS:

1. Transfer the jelly into a pastry bag fitted with a long, thin tip.

2. Poke a hole in the middle of each donut with a skewer or small knife. Fill each donut with jelly, about 2 teaspoons each.

SWEET TIPS: *If you don't have a 1½-inch cookie cutter, use a shape such as a heart or star. You can also use a shot glass.*

Donuts swell quite a bit while frying, so don't fret if they look flat to start with. They'll puff up.

VEGAN SPRINKLED DONUTS

How to impress a vegan. MAKES 20

FOR THE DONUTS:

1 cup all-purpose flour

½ cup sugar

1½ teaspoons baking powder

¼ teaspoon salt

¼ teaspoon ground nutmeg

pinch of ground cinnamon

½ cup soy milk

½ teaspoon apple cider vinegar

½ teaspoon vanilla extract

liquid egg replacer for 1 egg

¼ cup (½ stick) vegan butter (we like Earth Balance Vegan Buttery Sticks)

FOR THE GLAZE AND DECOR:

1 tablespoon soy milk

½ cup powdered sugar

½ cup sprinkles, the old-school rainbow kind

MAKE THE DONUTS:

1. Preheat the oven to 350°F. Spray a mini donut pan with cooking spray.

2. In a large bowl, sift together the flour, sugar, baking powder, salt, nutmeg, and cinnamon.

3. Combine the soy milk, vinegar, vanilla, egg replacer, and vegan butter in a medium saucepan. Heat over low heat just until the buttery stick is melted. The mixture is too hot if you cannot stick your finger in it without getting burned. Carefully test it if you're unsure.

4. Make a well in the center of the dry ingredients. Pour the warm wet ingredients into the well. Stir with a spatula until just combined.

5. Fit a pastry bag with a plain, large tip, preferably with a round opening of ⅛ inch or larger. Fill the pastry bag with the batter. Pipe the batter into the prepared pan, filling each well to the brim and working in batches if needed to get 20 total donuts.

6. Bake until the donuts spring back when touched but are not brown, about 12 minutes.

7. Allow to cool in the pan for 5 minutes, then turn out onto a cooling rack to cool completely.

MAKE THE GLAZE AND DECORATE:

1. Whisk together the soy milk and powdered sugar in a medium bowl.

2. Place the sprinkles in a small bowl. Lay a piece of waxed paper on the counter.

3. Dip each donut in the glaze, then into the sprinkles. Place on the waxed paper (sprinkles up!) to allow the glaze to harden.

4. Store in an airtight container for up to 2 days.

AZED CHOCOLATE DONUTS

36 donuts sounds like a lot? Just wait.   MAKES 36

THE DONUTS:

cup fine cake flour

¼ cup unsweetened cocoa powder

¾ teaspoon salt

½ cup sugar

1¼ teaspoons baking powder

1 large egg

¾ cup buttermilk

1 teaspoon vanilla extract

2 tablespoons unsalted butter, melted and slightly cooled

FOR THE GLAZE:

3 ounces semisweet chocolate baking squares

⅔ cup powdered sugar

2½ tablespoons milk

MAKE THE DONUTS:

1. Preheat the oven to 425°F. Spray a mini donut pan with cooking spray.

2. Sift together the flour, cocoa powder, salt, sugar, and baking powder in a large bowl.

3. In a medium bowl, lightly beat the egg. Add the buttermilk, vanilla, and melted butter.

4. Make a well in the center of the flour mixture. Pour the egg mixture into the well and mix with a spatula until combined.

5. Fit a pastry bag with a plain, large tip, preferably with a round opening of ⅛ inch or larger. Fill the pastry bag with the batter.

6. Pipe the batter into the prepared pan, filling each well three-quarters full. There will be batter left over. Set the pastry bag aside.

7. Bake for 5 minutes until the donuts spring back when touched. Allow to cool for 5 minutes in the pan, then transfer to a cutting board or cooling rack to cool completely. Re-spray and re-load the pan with more batter until all the batter is gone.

MAKE THE GLAZE:

1. Melt the chocolate over low heat in a small saucepan. In a medium bowl, whisk together the powdered sugar and milk. When the chocolate is melted, whisk in the milk mixture. Keeping the heat on low to prevent the chocolate from setting, hand dip the top of each donut in the glaze and swirl to coat. Place on a sheet of waxed paper to cool.

2. Store in an airtight container for 2 days. If they last that long.

SWEET TIPS: *It's nice to have a partner in the kitchen for the glazing. Because the glaze needs to remain over heat, it helps to stir it frequently while glazing the donuts.*

Cake flour tends to clump easily due to its fine texture. Sifting will help solve this problem.

CLASSIC BITES

The grand finale. These are the classic desserts you grew up enjoying at your grandma's house. We just took the liberty of miniaturizing them. These decadent little delights will bring back fond memories of Grandma's traditional cakes and pies and give them a modern twist. Serve these for dessert and you'll secure a special place in everyone's heart.

BLACK FOREST BIRTHDAY CAKE

A delicious way to turn one year older.   MAKES 12

FOR THE CAKES:

1 cup fine cake flour

1 teaspoon baking soda

¼ teaspoon baking powder

3 tablespoons unsweetened Dutch process cocoa powder

1 tablespoon espresso powder

¼ teaspoon salt

3 large eggs, at room temperature

1 cup sugar

½ teaspoon vanilla extract

1½ cups water

FOR THE SIMPLE SYRUP:

¼ cup sugar

½ cup water

2 tablespoons Kirsch

FOR THE KIRSCH WHIPPED CREAM:

3 cups cold heavy whipping cream

½ cup powdered sugar

4 tablespoons Kirsch

FOR ASSEMBLY:

2 cups coarsely chopped maraschino cherries

12 whole maraschino cherries, for garnish

MAKE THE CAKES:

1. Preheat the oven to 350°F. Generously spray a standard muffin pan with cooking spray. Cut little circles of waxed paper to fit in the bottom of each well. Place in the pan and spray the paper with cooking spray. This will ensure that the bottoms of the cakes do not stick.

2. Sift together the flour, baking soda, baking powder, cocoa powder, espresso powder, and salt.

3. In an electric mixer fitted with the whisk attachment, beat the eggs on medium-high speed until very frothy.

4. Set aside 2 tablespoons of the sugar. With the mixer running, gradually sprinkle in the remaining sugar and beat until combined. The mixture should look thick and fluffy and fall in a steady stream when you lift the whisk out of it. When it reaches this point, add the vanilla and beat to combine.

5. Change the mixer attachment to the paddle. With the mixer running on medium speed, add half the flour mixture and half the sugar you've set aside. Then add 1 cup water, then the remaining flour mixture and sugar, then ½ cup water, beating to combine after each addition.

6. Using a standard ice cream scoop, fill each well in the prepared pan three-quarters full.

7. Bake until a toothpick inserted into the center returns with few or no crumbs, 20 to 25 minutes.

8. Allow to cool for 10 minutes in the pan, or until safe to handle. Then remove from the pan and transfer to a cooling rack to cool completely. Thanks to the waxed paper in the bottom of each well, you can try turning the pan upside down and nudging them out that way.

MAKE THE SIMPLE SYRUP:

1. In a medium saucepan, combine the sugar and water over medium heat and bring to a boil.

2. Remove from the heat and allow to cool for 5 minutes. Stir in the Kirsch.

MAKE THE KIRSCH WHIPPED CREAM:

1. Chill the bowl and whisk attachment of your electric mixer for 30 minutes.

2. Beat the whipping cream on medium-high speed until soft peaks form, 2 to 3 minutes. With the mixer running, gradually sprinkle in the powdered sugar. Reduce the mixer speed to low and add the Kirsch. Beat until just combined.

ASSEMBLE THE CAKES:

1. Take a cake and slice it horizontally in 3 equal layers.

SWEET TIPS: K... is a clear, fruit-fla... brandy. It's a not-s... secret ingredient th... contributes to thi... cake's BIG taste. ... you can't find Kirsch... replace the syrup with chocolate glaze (see page 67) and layer with plain whipped cream.

2. Using a pastry brush, brush the top side of the smallest bottom layer with the simple syrup. Top this with a thin layer of the whipped cream, ¼ inch or less. Sprinkle 1 teaspoon of chopped cherries on top. Then top with another thin layer of whipped cream.

3. Place the middle piece of cake on top of the whipped cream. Brush the top of it with simple syrup, then add the whipped cream, then the cherries, then more whipped cream.

4. Place the last piece of cake on top. Frost the entire outside of the little cake with the whipped cream. Garnish with a whole cherry, if desired.

5. Turn on some music, and repeat for the remaining 11 cakes.

6. Store in the refrigerator in an airtight container for up to 2 days.

COOKIES 'N' CREAM CAKE

America's favorite cookie becomes your new favorite cake. MAKES 12

FOR THE CAKE:

2 ounces semisweet chocolate baking squares, chopped

3 tablespoons water

2 large eggs

1 cup all-purpose flour

½ teaspoon baking powder

½ teaspoon baking soda

¼ teaspoon salt

½ cup (1 stick) unsalted butter, at room temperature

½ cup plus 2 tablespoons sugar, divided

½ cup buttermilk, at room temperature

½ teaspoon vanilla extract

3 Oreo cookies, crushed

FOR THE OREO BUTTERCREAM:

1 cup (2 sticks) unsalted butter, at room temperature

3 cups powdered sugar

2 tablespoons heavy whipping cream

1 teaspoon vanilla extract

½ teaspoon salt

12 Oreos, crushed to fine crumbs

FOR THE GARNISH:

15 mini Oreos

MAKE THE CAKES:

1. Preheat the oven to 350°F. Generously spray a standard muffin pan with cooking spray. Cut little circles of waxed paper to fit in the bottom of each well. Place in the pan and spray the paper with cooking spray. This will ensure that the bottoms of the cakes do not stick.

2. In a small saucepan over low heat, combine the chocolate and water. Stir constantly until melted and smooth. Remove from the heat and set aside to cool.

3. Separate the egg yolks and egg whites. Set both aside.

4. Sift together the flour, baking powder, baking soda, and salt into a medium bowl.

5. Place the butter and ½ cup of the sugar in the bowl of an electric mixer fitted with the paddle attachment. Beat on medium speed until light and fluffy, 4 to 5 minutes.

6. Reduce the speed to medium and add the chocolate in a steady stream. Beat until combined. Add the egg yolks one at a time, incorporating after each.

7. With the mixer still running, add half of the flour mixture and beat until just combined. Add all of the buttermilk and vanilla and beat until just combined. Finally, add the remaining flour mixture and beat until combined.

8. Transfer the cake mixture into a large bowl. Set aside. Clean the mixer bowl and fit the mixer with the whisk attachment.

9. Place the egg whites in the mixer bowl and beat on high speed until soft peaks form. With the mixer running, add the remaining 2 tablespoons sugar and continue to beat until stiff peaks form.

10. Fold the egg whites into the cake batter with a spatula. Fold in the crushed cookies.

11. Using a standard ice cream scoop, fill each well in the prepared pan three-quarters full.

12. Bake until a toothpick inserted into the center returns with few or no crumbs, 20 to 23 minutes.

13. Allow to cool in the pan for 10 minutes, then remove as soon as safely possible. Transfer to a cooling rack to cool completely. Thanks to the waxed paper in the bottom of each well, you can try turning the pan upside down and nudging them out that way.

MAKE THE OREO BUTTERCREAM:

1. In an electric mixer fitted with the paddle attachment, combine the butter, sugar, and salt on medium speed. Watch it closely. After it's combined, beat for 3 more minutes.

2. With the mixer running, add the whipping cream and vanilla. Beat for 1 minute.

3. Reduce the speed to low. Add the cookie crumbs and beat until combined.

ASSEMBLE THE CAKES:

1. Take a little cake and slice it horizontally into 2 equal layers.

2. Place a dollop of frosting on top of the smaller bottom layer and spread evenly. Place the top layer on top.

3. Frost the entire cake with the Oreo buttercream.

4. Place a mini Oreo on top for garnish.

5. Crack open a bottle of your favorite wine, and repeat this for the remaining 11 mini cakes.

6. Store in an airtight container in the refrigerator for up to 2 days.

CARROT CAKE

This counts for at least one serving of vegetables, right?   MAKES 10

FOR THE CAKES:

1½ cups all-purpose flour

1 teaspoon baking soda

½ teaspoon salt

2 teaspoons ground cinnamon

1 teaspoon ground nutmeg

2 large eggs

¾ cup vegetable oil

1 cup brown sugar, packed

1 teaspoon vanilla extract

1¾ cups shredded carrot (about 3 carrots)

¼ cup peeled and grated apple
(we like Granny Smith)

½ cup unsweetened flaked coconut

½ cup finely chopped walnuts
(chopped in a food processor)

FOR THE CANDIED CARROT HEARTS:

1 carrot, preferably a thick one

½ cup sugar

½ cup water

FOR ASSEMBLY:

1 recipe Cream Cheese Frosting (page 137)

MAKE THE CAKE:

1. Preheat the oven to 350°F. Line a 12 x 18-inch rimmed baking sheet with waxed paper and spray the waxed paper with cooking spray.

2. Sift together the flour, baking soda, salt, cinnamon, and nutmeg in a medium bowl.

3. In a stand mixer fitted with the paddle attachment, lightly beat the eggs on low speed. Add the oil, brown sugar, and vanilla. Beat until combined. Gradually add the flour mixture and mix until combined. Mix in the shredded carrots, grated apple, coconut, and walnuts.

4. Pour the batter onto the prepared baking sheet and spread with a spatula until even. The batter should be about ½ inch thick. Bake for 18 minutes, rotating the pan halfway through. Allow to cool for 5 minutes in the pan, then turn out onto a cutting board to cool completely.

MAKE THE CANDIED CARROT HEARTS:

1. Take the fattest carrot and chop off the thicker top half. Using that top half and a great deal of caution, slice the carrot lengthwise into strips ideally ¹⁄₁₆ inch thick, starting on one side and working your way to the other. With a ½ inch heart-shaped cookie cutter, cut little carrot hearts out of each strip. You'll need at least 10, depending on how many you want on top of each mini cake.

2. Combine the sugar and water in a medium saucepan over medium heat. Bring to a boil, stirring occasionally. Add the carrot hearts and continue to boil for 10 minutes. Remove from the heat and allow to sit in the saucepan to cool for 10 minutes. Then transfer the hearts to a plate or cutting board to finish cooling.

ASSEMBLE THE CAKES:

1. When the cake has completely cooled, use a 3-inch biscuit cutter to cut out 20 circles.

2. Take half of the cake circles and place them flat-side down, rough-side up. With a small spatula, spread 1 tablespoon of frosting on each cake, avoiding the edges. Top each cake circle with the remaining cake circles, placing the flat side up. Spread the remaining frosting over each cake's top and sides.

3. Top each cake with a candied heart. Refrigerate in an airtight container for up to 3 days.

PERFECT PIE CRUST

Makes enough for 12 mini pies and pie toppers

½ cup (1 stick) cold unsalted butter

6 tablespoons cold shortening

2½ cups all-purpose flour

2 teaspoons salt

4 teaspoons sugar

6 to 8 tablespoons ice water

1. Dice the butter and shortening into ¼-inch pieces. Place in the freezer to chill.

2. Place the flour, salt, and sugar in a food processor and process to blend. Add the shortening and process until the mixture climbs the walls of the food processor. With the processor running, add the butter one piece at a time and process thoroughly.

3. With the processor running, add 1 tablespoon of ice water at a time until the mixture comes together in a ball and makes 2 laps around the processor bowl. Remove from the processor and divide the dough into 2 balls. Flatten each ball into a disc. Wrap each disc in plastic wrap.

4. Refrigerate for 30 minutes.

SWEET TIPS: *Leftover dough can be double wrapped in plastic wrap and refrigerated for 1 week, or frozen for up to 3 weeks.*

To make your pie crust vegan, simply replace the butter with vegan butter (we like Earth Balance Vegan Buttery Sticks) and replace the shortening with vegan shortening (we like Earth Balance Vegan Shortening Sticks).

When baking for vegan friends, grease the muffin pans with the vegan buttery sticks. Traditional cooking sprays are not vegan.

CHOCOLATE CHIPOTLE CREAM PIE

A twist on Aunt Jimma's classic.   MAKES 12

1 recipe Perfect Pie Crust dough (page 89)

1½ tablespoons all-purpose flour

1½ tablespoons unsweetened cocoa powder

¾ cup sugar

1½ egg yolks, reserving the whites for Perfect Mini Meringue

¾ cup PET milk

¼ cup whole milk

2 tablespoons butter

1 teaspoon vanilla extract

2 teaspoons adobo sauce from a can of chipotle chilies in adobo sauce

1 recipe Perfect Mini Meringue (page 135)

PRE-BAKE THE CRUSTS:

1. Preheat the oven to 350°F. Generously butter a standard muffin pan or spray with cooking spray.

2. On a thoroughly floured surface, roll out the pie crust to ³/₁₆ inch thick. Using a 3½-inch cookie cutter, cut 12 mini pie crusts. Re-form and re-roll the dough as needed, keeping plenty of flour on the work surface.

3. Carefully form the mini pie crusts into the wells of the muffin pan, creasing the edges with your fingers. Pierce the bottom of each crust with the tines of a fork.

4. Bake the crusts until lightly browned, about 20 minutes.

5. Remove from the oven and allow to cool slightly. Spin each crust in its well to ensure it is not stuck to the pan, then allow to cool completely.

MAKE THE FILLING AND BAKE THE PIES:

1. Meanwhile, in a large pot, mix together the flour, cocoa powder, and sugar.

2. Add the egg yolks, PET milk, whole milk, butter, vanilla, and adobo sauce.

3. Cook over low heat until thickened, constantly stirring with a whisk. When ready, the mixture should coat the back of a spoon and look similar to chocolate pudding. This should take about 35 minutes.

4. Preheat the oven to 350°F.

5. Pour the chocolate filling into the pre-baked pie crusts, filling to the brim. Allow to cool for 5 minutes.

6. Transfer the meringue into a pastry bag fitted with a flower tip and top each pie with meringue. Bake until the meringue is lightly browned, 10 to 15 minutes.

7. Allow to cool for a few minutes in the pan, then carefully place on cooling racks to cool completely.

8. Refrigerate in airtight container for up to 2 days.

SWEET TIPS: *Other canned evaporated milks are not the same thing as PET brand milk. PET is the best choice for this recipe, but in a pinch you can use other evaporated milk and still achieve delicious results.*

If 2 teaspoons chile sauce doesn't sound like much, trust us—it is.

BLACKBERRY LIME MERINGUE PIE

Well worth it. *VEGAN-FRIENDLY, MINUS THE MERINGUE* *MAKES 12*

1 recipe Perfect Pie Crust dough made with vegan butter and shortening (page 89)

FOR THE LIME CURD:

¾ cup lime juice

1 tablespoon grated lime zest

¾ cup sugar

pinch of salt

1½ tablespoons cornstarch dissolved in 1½ tablespoons cold water

1 tablespoon coconut milk

1 tablespoon vegan butter, cut into small pieces

FOR THE BLACKBERRY COMPOTE:

1 cup fruity red wine (Cabernet or Shiraz)

½ cup sugar

½ cup water

3 cups blackberries

1 recipe Perfect Mini Meringue (page 135)

PRE-BAKE THE CRUSTS:

1. Preheat the oven to 350°F. Generously butter a standard muffin pan or spray with cooking spray.

2. On a thoroughly floured surface, roll out the pie crust to ³/₁₆ inch thick. Using a 3½-inch cookie cutter, cut 12 mini pie crusts. Re-form and re-roll the dough as needed, keeping plenty of flour on the work surface.

3. Carefully form the mini pie crusts into the wells of the muffin pan, creasing the edges with your fingers.

4. Bake the crusts until lightly browned, about 20 minutes.

5. Remove from the oven and allow to cool.

MAKE THE LIME CURD:

1. Combine the lime juice and zest, sugar, and salt in a medium saucepan. Stir well over medium heat until the sugar is dissolved.

2. Add the cornstarch mixture and the coconut milk. Continue to cook and stir until the mixture begins to thicken and it just comes to a boil. Add the vegan butter, and continue stirring until the mixture is thick like pudding. Remove from the heat.

3. Transfer to a heatproof bowl and cover with plastic wrap so that the plastic wrap is in contact with the curd. Allow to cool.

MAKE THE BLACKBERRY COMPOTE:

1. Combine the wine, sugar, and water in a small saucepan over medium heat, stirring occasionally, until the mixture is reduced to about ½ cup liquid, about 20 minutes.

2. Remove from the heat and allow to cool for 5 minutes.

3. Gently stir in the berries and allow to cool completely.

ASSEMBLE THE PIES:

1. Place ½ tablespoon blackberry compote in the bottom of each pre-baked pie crust.

2. Top with the cooled lime curd and fill to just below the crust's edge (about 1½ tablespoons).

3. Refrigerate for 2 hours or overnight, leaving the pies in the muffin pan.

TOP WITH MERINGUE:

1. Preheat the oven to 350°F.

2. Pipe the meringue on top of the cold pies using a pastry bag with a large flower tip.

3. Bake until the meringue starts to brown, about 15 minutes.

4. Allow to cool for 5 minutes in the pan, then remove as soon as safely possible. Transfer to a cooling rack to cool completely.

5. Refrigerate in an airtight container for up to 2 days.

SWEET TIPS: *You'll likely have leftover blackberry compote. Use it as jam!*

APPLE PIE COOKIES

What will they think of next?   *MAKES ABOUT 24*

½ teaspoon ground cinnamon

⅛ teaspoon ground cardamom

¼ teaspoon ground allspice

2 tablespoons brown sugar

¼ cup plus 2 tablespoons
   granulated sugar, divided

1 tablespoon lemon juice

1 teaspoon vanilla extract

4 large apples (we like Granny Smith)

2 recipes Perfect Pie Crust
   dough (page 89)

¼ cup soy milk

1. Preheat the oven to 350°F. Line two rimmed baking sheets with parchment paper and spray the paper with cooking spray.

2. Combine the cinnamon, cardamom, allspice, brown sugar, 2 tablespoons of the granulated sugar, and the lemon juice and vanilla in a large bowl.

3. Peel the apples. With each apple upright, slice ¼-inch-thick slices vertically through the apple, avoiding the core. Your goal is to get flat apple slices. Use a 1½-inch scalloped cookie cutter to cut the apple slices into discs.

4. Place the apple discs in the bowl with the sugar-spice mixture and toss to combine.

5. Roll out the pie crust to ⅛ inch thick. Cut out 12 circles with the 1½-inch scalloped cookie cutter, and 12 with a 2-inch scalloped cookie cutter. The larger ones will be the bottom of each cookie, the smaller ones the top. In the center of each smaller top piece, use a tiny decorative cookie cutter (about

½-inch; we like hearts) to cut out a vent. Place the dough circles on the prepared baking sheets and refrigerate for 5 minutes.

SWEET TIPS: *You can prepare the second tray of cookies while the first one is baking. Store in the fridge until tray #1 is done baking.*

6. Work with 1 sheet of dough rounds at a time. Take a larger circle and place it on a floured surface. Spread a little water around the edges with your fingers. This will help seal the cookies. Center an apple disc on top of the bottom crust. Place a smaller top crust on top. Using your fingers, seal the bottom crust to the top by folding the bottom layer up and over the top and smashing them together around the apple disc. Go back and imprint the edge with the tines of a fork for a decorative look.

7. When the cookie is assembled, return it to the baking sheet (making sure the sheet is still amply sprayed with cooking spray). Using a pastry brush, brush a little soy milk over the top and sprinkle with a little of the remaining ¼ cup sugar.

8. Repeat for the remaining cookies until all are assembled and ready to bake.

9. Bake 1 sheet at a time, until the cookies are puffed up and lightly browned, about 25 minutes

10. Allow to cool for 5 minutes on the pan, then transfer to a cooling rack to cool completely.

11. Store in an airtight container for up to 2 days.

ANGEL FOOD CAKE WITH VANILLA STRAWBERRIES

So sinful, it's heavenly.   MAKES 6 OR 12, DEPENDING ON THE PAN

FOR THE STRAWBERRY TOPPING:
1 pint fresh strawberries
½ vanilla bean, split lengthwise
1 tablespoon sugar

FOR THE CAKE:
1¾ cups sugar
1 cup fine cake flour, sifted
¼ teaspoon salt

12 large egg whites, at room temperature
⅓ cup warm water
1 teaspoon vanilla extract
1½ teaspoons cream of tartar

FOR THE WHIPPED CREAM:
¾ cup cold heavy whipping cream
2 tablespoons powdered sugar
½ teaspoon vanilla extract

MAKE THE STRAWBERRY TOPPING:

1. Slice the strawberries and place in a medium bowl, preferably one with a lid.

2. Scrape the vanilla bean on top of the strawberries. Discard the pod.

3. Add the sugar and stir. Refrigerate for a couple hours to allow the flavors to mingle and the strawberries to release their juices.

MAKE THE CAKES:

1. Preheat the oven to 350°F. Spray a mini Bundt pan with cooking spray.

2. In a food processor, process the sugar for 2 minutes. This will create a superfine sugar that is better for this cake.

3. Place half of the sugar in a small bowl and set aside.

4. Sift together the cake flour, salt, and remaining half of the sugar in a medium bowl.

5. In an electric mixer fitted with the whisk attachment, combine the egg whites, water, vanilla extract, and cream of tartar. Beat on medium speed until combined, then increase the speed to medium-high. Gradually sprinkle in the reserved sugar and beat until medium peaks form. The mixture should not be very foamy. Remove the bowl from the mixer.

6. With a spatula, gently fold in one-quarter of the flour mixture at a time until incorporated.

7. Using a 2-inch ice cream scoop, fill each well of the prepared pan to just below the brim.

8. Bake until the tops are lightly browned and a toothpick inserted into the center returns with no crumbs, 20 to 25 minutes.

9. Allow to cool for 5 minutes in the pan, then turn the cakes out onto a cooling rack to cool completely.

MAKE THE WHIPPED CREAM:

1. Chill the whisk attachment and bowl of an electric mixer. Beat the whipping cream until soft peaks form. With the mixer running, add the powdered sugar and vanilla. Beat until stiff peaks form and it looks like whipped cream.

2. Transfer into a pastry bag with a flower tip for the prettiest cakes.

ASSEMBLE THE CAKES:

1. Top each cake with strawberry topping then a dollop of whipped cream from the pastry bag.

2. You can store all components separately in airtight containers (with the strawberries and whipped cream in the fridge) for up to 2 days.

SWEET TIPS: *If you have any around, add 2 tablespoons of chopped fresh basil to the strawberry topping for an extra YUM factor.*

There are two kinds of mini Bundt/angel food cake pans available: 6 well (slightly larger) and 12 well (smaller). Either will work just fine for this recipe.

WINE & CHOCOLATE LAVA CAKES

Pairs well with life.   MAKES 9

1½ tablespoons unsweetened cocoa powder

2 tablespoons all-purpose flour

¼ cup granulated sugar, divided

¼ cup (½ stick) plus 1 tablespoon unsalted butter

7 ounces semisweet chocolate baking squares

¼ cup Merlot

3 large eggs, whites and yolks separated

¼ cup powdered sugar, for dusting

1. Preheat the oven to 350°F. Spray 9 wells of a mini Bundt pan with cooking spray.

2. Sift together the cocoa powder, flour, and 2 tablespoons of the granulated sugar in a small bowl.

3. Place the butter and baker's chocolate in a small saucepan. Heat over low heat until melted and combined. Remove from the heat and add the Merlot, the remaining 2 tablespoons granulated sugar, and the egg yolks. Stir gently to combine. Keep a close eye on the eggs to make sure they do not scramble.

4. In an electric mixer fitted with the whisk attachment, beat the egg whites until foamy, about 1 minute. Add about 2 tablespoons of the cocoa powder mixture and beat until soft peaks form.

5. Remove the bowl from the mixer. By hand, fold in half of the melted chocolate mixture, then half of the cocoa powder mixture. Then fold in the

remaining melted chocolate mixture, and finally the remaining cocoa powder mixture.

6. Fill the wells of the mini Bundt pan to the brim.

7. Bake for 10 minutes, and do not turn the pan. The cakes will be firm on the outside and gooey on the inside.

8. Cool for 3 minutes in the pan, and then turn out onto a cooling rack to cool completely. Dust with powdered sugar using a sifter. Wait at least 5 minutes to eat one (we know this may be difficult), as the centers are very gooey and hot! Serve with the remaining Merlot.

9. Store in an airtight container for up to 3 days.

SWEET TIPS: *If you would rather not have a "lava" center and just want a moist chocolate cake, add 2 minutes to the baking time.*

For the wine, you can buy a traditional 750ml bottle and drink the 90 percent of it you don't use to bake. Or, you can purchase a smaller bottle or box just for cooking. We like the mini Bota Box wines.

KIWI UPSIDE-DOWN CAKE

Making pineapples jealous since 2012. MAKES 12

1 cup unsweetened shredded coconut

6 teaspoons (2 tablespoons) brown sugar

2 gold kiwis

½ cup (1 stick) unsalted butter

½ cup sugar

1 large egg

1½ cups all-purpose flour

2 teaspoons baking powder

¾ cup orange juice

1. Preheat the oven to 350°F. Line a rimmed baking sheet with parchment paper. Spray a standard muffin pan with cooking spray.

2. Spread the coconut on the prepared baking sheet and toast until lightly browned. Watch it closely, as this only takes a few minutes.

3. Drop ½ teaspoon of the brown sugar into the bottom of each well in the muffin pan.

4. Peel and slice the kiwis. You need 6 slices from each kiwi, so slice accordingly. Place a kiwi slice on top of the brown sugar in each well.

5. In an electric mixer, beat the butter and sugar on medium speed until creamy but not fluffy. Add the egg and beat until combined.

6. With the mixer running, gradually add the flour. Add the baking powder, and then the orange juice. Beat until all the ingredients are incorporated.

7. Using a standard ice cream scoop, fill each well of the muffin pan to just below the brim. Top with the toasted coconut.

8. Bake until a toothpick inserted into the center returns with no crumbs, 18 to 20 minutes.

9. Allow to cool in the pan for 5 minutes. Then place a cooling rack on top of the muffin pan. Flip the whole thing over so the cooling rack is on the bottom. Lift the muffin tin off the cakes. Allow to cool completely on the cooling rack.

10. Store in an airtight container for up to 2 days.

SWEET TIPS: *If you can't find gold kiwis, the green ones will make beautiful cakes, too.*

MINI OLIVE OIL CAKE

Simple. Rich. Perfection.   MAKES 6 OR 12, DEPENDING ON THE SIZE OF THE PAN

⅔ cup cake flour

½ teaspoon salt

½ teaspoon baking powder

2 large whole eggs

1 large egg yolk

½ cup granulated sugar

1 packed teaspoon grated orange zest

1 teaspoon anise extract

½ cup extra-virgin olive oil

¼ cup powdered sugar, for dusting

1. Preheat the oven to 325°F. Spray a mini Bundt pan with cooking spray.

2. Sift together the flour, salt, and baking powder in a medium bowl.

3. In an electric mixer fitted with the whisk attachment, beat the whole eggs, egg yolk, granulated sugar, orange zest, and anise extract on medium speed until foamy.

4. With the mixer running, gradually add the oil in a steady stream and mix until combined.

5. Add the flour mixture gradually, adding one-third of it at a time. Mix until just combined.

6. Fill each well in the prepared pan two-thirds full. The cakes will puff up a bit.

7. Bake until lightly browned and a toothpick inserted into the center returns with no crumbs, about 20 minutes.

8. Allow to cool for 5 minutes in the pan, then turn out onto cooling racks to cool completely.

9. Using a sifter, dust the cakes with powdered sugar.

10. Store in an airtight container for up to 2 days.

FANCY STUFF

It's time to get serious. These baking projects will test your skills, and we're confident you'll get delicious results. There's everything from delicate mini cannoli to boozy tiraminiscule, and you're certain to impress your friends with your newfound expertise. You can do this. You are a baking ninja.

STRAWBERRY CREAM ÉCLAIRS

Fancy never looked so tiny. MAKES 20

FOR THE ÉCLAIRS:

¼ cup whole milk

¼ cup water

¼ cup (½ stick) unsalted butter

½ teaspoon salt

½ cup all-purpose flour

2 large eggs

FOR THE VANILLA CREAM:

1 vanilla bean, split lengthwise

1 cup cold heavy whipping cream

2 tablespoons powdered sugar

FOR THE BERRY FILLING:

2 cups strawberries, finely chopped

1 tablespoon sugar

2 teaspoons finely chopped fresh mint
or basil (choose your own path here)

½ cup powdered sugar, for dusting

MAKE THE ÉCLAIRS:

1. Preheat the oven to 400°F. Line two baking sheets with parchment paper and spray the paper with cooking spray.

2. Combine the milk, water, butter, and salt in a medium saucepan. Heat over medium-high heat, stirring constantly, until combined. Remove from the heat.

3. Add the flour and stir until combined. Return the pan to medium-high heat and cook for 4 minutes, stirring constantly, then remove from the heat.

4. Transfer the mixture to an electric mixer fitted with the paddle attachment. Mix on medium speed for 1 minute, then add the eggs one at a time. Make sure the first egg is incorporated before you add the second one.

5. Transfer the mixture into a pastry bag fitted with a plain ½-inch tip.

6. Pipe éclairs about 2½ inches long onto the prepared baking sheets, about 10 per sheet.

7. Bake until golden brown, about 20 minutes. Allow to cool for a few minutes on the baking sheet, then transfer to a cooling rack to cool completely.

MAKE THE VANILLA CREAM:

1. Chill the bowl and whisk attachment of an electric mixer for 30 minutes.

2. Scrape the vanilla bean into the mixer bowl. Discard the pod.

3. Add the whipping cream. Beat on medium-high speed until soft peaks form. With the mixer running, gradually add the powdered sugar and beat on medium-high speed until stiff peaks form.

4. Transfer the whipped cream into a pastry bag fitted with a large, plain tip. Refrigerate until ready to use.

MAKE THE BERRY FILLING:

1. Place the strawberries in a medium bowl. Add the mint or basil.

2. Add the sugar and stir. Cover and refrigerate for 1 hour.

ASSEMBLE THE ÉCLAIRS:

1. When the éclairs have completely cooled, slice each one in half lengthwise horizontally. Set each top next to its bottom.

2. Pipe the vanilla cream onto each bottom. Top the cream with the berry filling.

3. Replace the éclair tops. Sift powdered sugar over the tops.

4. Store in an airtight container for up to 1 day.

CANNOLI

A tiny taste of Italy.   VEGAN-FRIENDLY   MAKES 20

FOR THE CANNOLI SHELLS:

2 tablespoons warm water

½ teaspoon liquid egg replacer

2 tablespoons vegan butter
(we like Earth Balance)

2 tablespoons plus 2 teaspoons sugar

½ teaspoon grated orange zest

¼ teaspoon almond extract

¼ cup all-purpose flour

FOR THE FILLING:

¼ cup vegan butter

¼ cup vegan shortening (we
like Earth Balance)

1½ cups powdered sugar, plus
more for dusting, sifted

2 tablespoons vegan sour cream

1 teaspoon vanilla extract

2 tablespoons powdered soy milk

½ cup mini vegan chocolate chips,
plus more for decorating

MAKE THE CANNOLI SHELLS:

1. Preheat the oven to 375°F. Line two rimmed baking sheets with parchment paper and spray the paper with cooking spray. Find an object in your kitchen that is about ½ inch in diameter. You will use this to roll the cannoli later.

2. Add the warm water to the egg replacer in a small bowl. Stir and set aside.

3. In an electric mixer fitted with the paddle attachment, beat the butter and sugar on medium speed until fluffy.

4. Reduce the mixer speed to low and add the egg replacer.

5. Add the orange zest and almond extract and beat until incorporated. Gradually add the flour. Mix until the flour is fully incorporated and the mixture is smooth.

6. Take 1 tablespoon of the dough and place it on a prepared baking sheet. Spread the dough into a circle just under ⅛ inch thick. Repeat to fill the first baking sheet

7. Bake until the edges are just browned, 5 to 6 minutes. It's important to just bake one sheet at a time. While the first sheet is in the oven, you can prepare the second sheet with the dough.

8. Allow to cool on the sheet for 1 minute. Then take your ½-inch diameter object and wrap the dough around it to form a tube. The dough will still be hot, so be careful. Hold in place for about 20 seconds, then slide off the tube onto a cooling rack to cool completely. If the shells unroll, pinch them back together with your fingers for a few seconds.

9. Continue baking one sheet at a time until you have used all the dough.

MAKE THE FILLING:

1. While the cannoli shells are cooling, in an electric mixer fitted with the paddle attachment, combine the vegan butter, vegan shortening, powdered sugar, sour cream, and vanilla. Mix on medium speed until combined, about 2 minutes.

2. With the mixer running, gradually add the soy milk powder and beat until combined.

3. Reduce the mixer speed to low and add the mini chocolate chips.

4. Transfer the filling into a pastry bag fitted with a long, thin tip. Fill each cannoli. If desired, dip the end of each cannoli into more mini chocolate chips.

5. Cannoli are best served the day they are made. If you must store them, keep them in an airtight container at room temperature.

TIRAMINISCULE

A tiny, boozy treat. MAKES 12

FOR THE LADY FINGER CAKE:

3 large eggs, at room temperature, whites and yolks separated

5 tablespoons granulated sugar, divided

½ teaspoon vanilla extract

½ cup fine cake flour, sifted

¼ cup powdered sugar, for dusting

FOR THE ESPRESSO GLAZE:

8 ounces strong brewed coffee

2 ounces Scotch

1 teaspoon unsweetened cocoa powder

FOR THE TIRAMISU CREAM:

6 large eggs, at room temperature, whites and yolks separated

3 tablespoons sugar

1 pound (16 ounces) mascarpone cheese, at room temperature

2 ounces Scotch

FOR ASSEMBLY:

4 tablespoons unsweetened cocoa powder

1 tablespoon pumpkin pie spice

MAKE THE LADY FINGER CAKE:

1. Preheat the oven to 350°F. Line a rimmed baking sheet with parchment paper (bottom and sides) and spray the paper with cooking spray.

2. In an electric mixer fitted with the paddle attachment, beat the egg yolks and 2 tablespoons of the granulated sugar on medium-high speed. Beat until the mixture is thick and a light yellow color, about 5 minutes. Test the consistency by turning the mixer off and lifting the paddle out of the batter. The batter should flow back into the bowl in a steady ribbon.

3. Turn the mixer back on to low speed. Mix in the vanilla.

4. Transfer the batter to a large bowl. Sift the flour over the batter, but do not mix it in. Just let it sit.

5. Clean the mixer bowl and fit the mixer with the whisk attachment. Beat the egg whites on medium-high speed until foamy.

6. With the mixer running, gradually sprinkle the remaining 3 tablespoons granulated sugar into the egg whites. Beat until stiff peaks form.

7. Fold one-third of the egg whites into the cake batter with a spatula, incorporating after each addition.

8. Spread the batter onto prepared baking sheet to ⅜ inch thick. It may not take up your whole sheet, and it may be irregular in shape. That's OK because you're going to cut it up later. Use a sifter to dust the entire cake with the powdered sugar.

9. Bake until the cake is spongy to the touch and only barely browned, 8 to 10 minutes

10. Use the parchment paper to lift the cake off the baking sheet and onto a cooling rack to cool completely.

MAKE THE ESPRESSO GLAZE:

1. Place the coffee in a large bowl with a flat bottom, if possible. Stir in the Scotch and cocoa powder. Set aside to cool.

CUT THE LADYFINGER CAKES:

1. Place the ladyfinger cake on the counter, leaving the parchment paper intact on the bottom side. Cut out 12 circles with a 2-inch cookie cutter, and cut out 12 more circles with a 2¾-inch cookie cutter. Set aside.

MAKE THE TIRAMISU CREAM:

1. In an electric mixer fitted with the paddle attachment, beat the egg yolks and sugar until creamy and white, 2 to 3 minutes.

2. With the mixer running, add the mascarpone cheese and Scotch. Beat until combined.

3. Transfer to a large bowl and set aside.

4. Clean the mixer bowl and fit the mixer with the whisk attachment. Beat the egg whites on high speed until soft peaks form.

5. Gently fold the egg whites into the mascarpone mixture with a spatula. Be careful, and mix only enough to incorporate the egg whites.

6. Transfer the tiramisu cream into a pastry bag fitted with a large flower tip.

ASSEMBLE THE TIRAMINISCULES:

1. Line a standard 12-well muffin pan with fancy paper liners. We like the pretty ones from Wilton that look like daisies and tulips, but use your own artistic license here.

2. Pick up a 2-inch cake circle. Drop it quickly into the espresso glaze with the sugared side UP. Then flip it over and drop it into a cupcake liner with the sugared side DOWN and espresso side UP. This will allow the espresso

to trickle down as the desserts chill in the fridge overnight. Do this for the remaining 2-inch circles.

3. Pipe a layer of tiramisu cream on top of each 2-inch circle, about ½ inch thick.

4. Repeat the dipping process for the 2¾-inch cake circles and place them the same way on top of the layer of cream.

5. Pipe another layer of cream on top.

6. Mix the cocoa powder and pumpkin pie spice in a small bowl. Then use a small sifter to sift a generous coating onto each tiraminiscule.

7. Cover loosely with foil. Refrigerate overnight in the pan.

8. Best served the following day.

> **SWEET TIPS:** *This recipe contains raw egg and booze. Lots of it. For that reason it should not be offered to expectant mothers, young children, the elderly, or anyone with a compromised immune system. In other words, don't take these to someone's 1st or 80th birthday party.*
>
> *If you dig around in your kitchen, I bet you can find items that are the right diameter circles to cut the cakes. Shot glasses, Mason jars, measuring cups, juice glasses—most anything would work.*

VERRY BERRY CHEESECAKES

That "Factory" has nothin' on us! MAKES 12

FOR THE GRAHAM CRACKER CRUST:

1½ cups fine graham cracker crumbs

⅓ cup unsalted butter, melted and slightly cooled

FOR THE FILLING:

2 large eggs, at room temperature, whites and yolks separated

2 (8-ounce) packages cream cheese, at room temperature

1 cup sugar

¼ cup sour cream

1 teaspoon vanilla extract

FOR THE TOPPING:

½ cup blueberries

½ cup blackberries

½ cup raspberries

½ cup strawberries

MAKE THE CRUST:

1. Preheat the oven to 375°F. Spray a mini cheesecake pan with cooking spray. Ours is by Chicago Metallic and has removable plates in the bottom of each well. This is incredibly helpful in removing the cheesecakes after baking. If you do not have a mini cheesecake pan, you can improvise by using a standard 12-well muffin pan and paper liners.

2. Place the graham cracker crumbs in a medium bowl. Drizzle the melted butter over the crumbs and stir with a spatula until combined. Sprinkle about 1 tablespoon of the crust mixture in the bottom of each well in the prepared pan. Compact it with your fingers to be ¼ inch thick on the bottom, and create a little lip that's about ⅛ inch thick around the edges. This will provide a good base for the cheesecakes and help to contain the filling.

MAKE THE FILLING:

1. In an electric mixer fitted with the whisk attachment, beat the egg whites on high speed until soft peaks form. Transfer to a medium bowl and set aside.

2. Fit the mixer with paddle attachment. Beat the egg yolks and cream cheese on medium speed until almost combined, 2 to 3 minutes.

3. Stop the mixer and gently fold in the egg whites with a spatula.

4. Turn the mixer back on to medium speed, sprinkle in the sugar, and beat until combined. Add the sour cream and vanilla and beat until combined.

5. Using a 2-inch ice cream scoop, put one level scoop of filling into each well on top of the crust.

6. Bake until the filling looks slightly firm, about 20 minutes. It should have little or no jiggle to it.

7. Allow to cool for 1 hour in the pan, preferably with the pan on a cooling rack.

8. Transfer the pan to the refrigerator and cool for 1 hour, uncovered.

MAKE THE TOPPING:

1. Place ¼ cup of each type of berry in the bowl of a food processor. Pulse until a smooth compote has formed. Set aside.

2. Take the remaining berries and chop the larger ones to a size that will work as a garnish. The blueberries and raspberries will not need to be chopped, but large blackberries and strawberries could be cut in half.

ASSEMBLE THE CHEESECAKES:

1. After the cakes have cooled for 1 hour in the fridge, carefully remove them from the pan by pushing up the bottom removable plates.

2. Place the cheesecakes on the intended serving tray. It's best not to move them after you've topped them if you can avoid it.

3. Top each cheesecake with the berry compote and then with the remaining whole berries.

4. Refrigerate in an airtight container for up to 1 day.

PIECAKEN

You'll be the hero of any party.   MAKES 4

1 recipe Perfect Pie Crust dough (page 89)

FOR THE CHERRY FILLING:

2 cups coarsely chopped pitted cherries

1 tablespoon lemon juice

pinch of ground cinnamon

1 tablespoon sugar

FOR THE CHOCOLATE CAKE BATTER:

⅓ cup unsweetened Dutch process cocoa
    powder, plus more for the pans

¾ cup all-purpose flour

¾ cup sugar

¾ teaspoon baking soda

½ teaspoon baking powder

½ teaspoon salt

1 large egg

⅓ cup low-fat buttermilk

⅓ cup warm water

1½ tablespoons vegetable oil

1 teaspoon vanilla extract

FOR THE CHOCOLATE FROSTING:

1 cup powdered sugar

2 tablespoons unsweetened cocoa powder

pinch of salt

5 ounces semisweet chocolate
    baking squares

6 tablespoons unsalted butter,
    at room temperature

6 ounces cream cheese

⅓ cup sour cream

FOR THE GARNISH:

4 fresh cherries, stems and pits intact

PREPARE YOURSELF FOR BAKING:

1. Clear your afternoon.

2. Put on your least favorite shirt and apron. Roll up the sleeves of said shirt.

3. Refrigerate the pie crust dough for at least 30 minutes.

MAKE THE CHERRY FILLING:

1. Combine the cherries, lemon juice, cinnamon, and sugar in a medium bowl. Toss to combine. Allow to sit for 20 minutes, tossing occasionally.

2. Drain the excess juice out of the cherries using a fine-mesh strainer. There is such a thing as a pie that's too juicy, and cherries can be problematic in this department.

BAKE THE PIES:

1. Preheat the oven to 350°F. Spray 5 wells of a standard muffin pan with cooking spray. This recipe makes 4 Piecakens, but we're hedging our bets and making 5 cherry pies just to be safe. Worst-case scenario, you eat a perfect little cherry pie because it's extra.

2. Roll out the pie crust to ⅜ inch thick and cut individual crusts with a 4-inch fluted tart pan. Fill each prepared well with a mini bottom crust.

3. Fill each pie crust with a heaping serving of cherry filling, about 2 tablespoons each. You want the pile of cherries to rise above the edge of the muffin pan.

4. Cut a top crust for each mini pie using the same 4-inch tart cutter. Cut a little hole (like a decorative heart) in each top crust to allow for juice to escape while baking. Trim any excess crust and fasten each top crust to its bottom by squishing it with your fingers. Any leftover pie crust you have can be double wrapped in plastic wrap and frozen.

5. Bake the pies for 25 minutes, rotating the pan halfway through. Allow to cool in the pan for 5 minutes, and then remove from pan as soon as safely possible. Transfer to a cooling rack to cool completely. Turn off the oven.

MAKE THE CHOCOLATE CAKE:

1. In an electric mixer fitted with the paddle attachment, combine the cocoa powder, flour, sugar, baking soda, baking powder, and salt. Mix on medium speed until combined.

2. Combine the egg, buttermilk, warm water, vegetable oil, and vanilla in a medium bowl.

3. Add the wet ingredients to the dry ingredients and mix on medium speed until fully combined, about 3 minutes.

4. Preheat the oven again to 350°F. Spray four small baking dishes, about 4 inches in diameter and 2½ inches tall, with cooking spray. Place the baking dishes on a rimmed baking sheet.

5. Using a standard ice cream scoop, put a full scoop of cake batter in each baking dish. Carefully and evenly place each pie on top of the batter. Cover each pie with the remaining cake batter, filling the baking dish to just below the brim.

6. Bake until a toothpick inserted along the edge returns with no crumbs, about 35 minutes.

7. Allow to cool for 5 minutes, then carefully turn each Piecaken upside down and out of the baking dish. Trim any irregular bumps or edges with a sharp knife. Allow to cool for a couple hours.

MAKE THE FROSTING:

1. Sift together the powdered sugar, cocoa powder, and salt in a medium bowl.

2. Melt the chocolate in a small saucepan over low heat. Set aside to cool slightly.

3. Combine the butter and cream cheese in an electric mixer fitted with the paddle attachment and beat on medium speed until combined and smooth, about 1 minute.

4. Gradually add the cocoa powder mixture and beat until combined. Gradually add the melted chocolate in a thin stream and beat until combined. Add the sour cream and beat until combined.

ASSEMBLE THE PIECAKENS:

1. Using a generous spatula's worth of frosting, frost each Piecaken, starting at the top and working your way down. Top each with a whole cherry for garnish.

2. Now it's time for the moment of glory. Take your sharpest knife and slice through the middle of a Piecaken (avoiding the cherry) to reveal the pie suspended inside.

3. Eat it. And take a load off, it's been a long day of baking.

ALMOND BABY BEAR CLAWS

As tasty as they are adorable.   MAKES 18

FOR THE BABY BEAR CLAW DOUGH:
1½ cups cold unsalted butter
5 cups all-purpose flour, divided
1 packet (2¼ teaspoons) active dry yeast
1¼ cups half-and-half
¼ cup sugar
¼ teaspoon salt
1 large egg

FOR THE FILLING:
1 large egg white
¾ cup powdered sugar, sifted
½ cup almond paste, cubed
1 tablespoon water

FOR BAKING AND ASSEMBLY:
1 large egg white
sugar, for sprinkling
sliced almonds, for topping

MAKE THE BABY BEAR CLAW DOUGH:

1. Dice the butter into ¼-inch pieces. Place 3 cups of the flour in a large bowl. Toss the butter in the flour to coat and place in the refrigerator.

2. In a second large bowl, combine the remaining 2 cups flour and the yeast. Make a well in the center.

3. In a small saucepan, combine the half-and-half, sugar, and salt over medium-low heat. Using a candy thermometer, heat the mixture to 120 to 130°F. Pour the warm half-and-half mixture into the well in the center of the flour-yeast mixture. Add the egg, and quickly stir with a spatula until smooth, making

sure the egg doesn't begin to cook. Stir in the butter-flour mixture until just combined.

4. Generously dust your kitchen counter with flour. Roll the dough into a 12 x 20-inch rectangle. Working from the short side, fold the dough into thirds. Turn the dough 90 degrees and repeat. Roll it out to a 12 x 20-inch rectangle, then fold into thirds. Roll the dough and fold it into thirds one more time.

5. Wrap the dough in plastic wrap and refrigerate for at least 4 hours. You can make the dough up to 1 day ahead and refrigerate it overnight.

WHEN THE DOUGH IS READY, MAKE THE FILLING:

1. In an electric mixer fitted with the whisk attachment, beat the egg white on medium-high speed until foamy. With the mixer running, gradually add the powdered sugar. Add the almond paste and water and beat until combined and smooth.

FORM THE BABY BEAR CLAWS:

1. Spray two rimmed baking sheets with cooking spray. Cut the cold dough in half.

2. Roll out each half to a 12-inch square. Cut each square into 3 equal strips that are about 12 x 4 inches.

3. Spread a few tablespoons of filling along the center of each strip. Fold the strips in half and seal all the edges by mashing the dough together with your fingers. Cut each strip into 3 equal pieces. Place the baby bear claws on the

prepared baking sheets with the long, newly sealed edges toward you. Using kitchen scissors or a small knife, make 4 small cuts along the long front edge to form "claws."

4. Cover and let rise for 1 hour in a warm place.

BAKE!:

1. Preheat the oven to 375°F.

2. Make an egg wash by beating the egg white with a fork in a small bowl until foamy. Brush over the baby bear claws with a pastry brush.

3. Sprinkle each baby bear claw with sugar and almonds.

4. Bake until lightly browned, about 15 minutes.

5. Allow to cool for 5 minutes on the baking sheet, then transfer to a cooling rack to cool completely.

6. Store in an airtight container for up to 2 days.

FROSTINGS, FILLINGS, TOPPINGS, AND DRIZZLES

You've heard the phrase "icing on the cake"? Well, here it is. Add these tools to your repertoire to take your desserts from decent to decadent.

VERY BEST BUTTERCREAM

Consider yourself spoiled. VEGAN-FRIENDLY

½ cup vegan shortening, at room temperature (we like Spectrum)

½ cup (1 stick) vegan butter at room temperature (we like Earth Balance Buttery Sticks)

3½ cups powdered sugar

2½ teaspoons vanilla extract

¼ cup soy milk

1. Get out your trusty kitchen timer. Place the vegan shortening and butter in an electric mixer fitted with the paddle attachment. Beat on medium until completely combined, about 3 minutes. Add the powdered sugar and beat until combined, about 3 minutes. Add the vanilla and soy milk. Beat for 7 whole minutes.

SWEET TIPS: *We really do prefer vegan buttercream to dairy-based buttercream.*

Vegan shortening and buttery sticks can be found at stores such as Whole Foods.

EXTRA-SPECIAL FROSTING

The honey and delicate spice are what make this frosting so special.

½ cup vegan shortening, at room temperature (we like Earth Balance Vegan Shortening)

½ cup (1 stick) vegan butter sticks, at room temperature (we like Earth Balance Buttery Sticks)

3½ cups powdered sugar

2 teaspoons vanilla extract

¼ cup soy milk

¼ cup honey

1 tablespoon ground cinnamon

1. Get out your trusty kitchen timer. In an electric mixer fitted with the paddle attachment, beat the vegan shortening and butter on medium speed until completely combined, about 3 minutes. Add the powdered sugar and beat until combined, about 3 minutes. Add the vanilla and soy milk, and beat for 5 minutes. Add the honey and cinnamon. Beat for 2 minutes.

SWEET TIP: *Extra-special frosting is vegan-friendly, but sticklers should replace the honey with agave nectar.*

CLASSIC STREUSEL

A great topping for muffins and coffee cakes.

½ cup all-purpose flour

3 tablespoons cold unsalted butter, diced

¼ cup brown sugar, packed

½ teaspoon vanilla extract

1. Combine all the ingredients in a large bowl and combine with your fingers until the mixture looks like sand. Cover and refrigerate for 30 minutes before using.

2. Before baking muffins or coffee cakes, dust them generously with the streusel. It's OK if the streusel looks messy and spills down the sides of your baked goods.

SWEET TIPS: *You can switch out the vanilla extract for lemon or almond extract to better match the flavors you're using in your muffins or coffee cakes.*

PERFECT MINI MERINGUE

No matter what you've heard, this isn't impossible.   *MAKES ENOUGH FOR 24 MINI PIES*

4 large egg whites, at room temperature

¼ teaspoon cream of tartar

¼ teaspoon salt

5 tablespoons sugar

1. In an electric mixer fitted with the whisk attachment, beat the egg whites until foamy.

2. Add the cream of tartar and salt and beat to mix.

3. Continue to beat at a high speed, adding 1 tablespoon of sugar at a time. Beat well after each addition and continue to add sugar until stiff peaks form, about 5 minutes.

4. Spread or pipe meringue onto each mini pie, making sure the edges are covered and sealed. Then pile high in the center.

SWEET TIPS: *For the prettiest meringues, use a pastry bag fitted with a flower tip to pipe the meringue on top.*

If you accidentally get any egg yolk in with your whites, remove it. The meringue will not turn out if there is yolk involved.

FALL SPICE GLAZE

Great for scookies and muffins!

½ cup powdered sugar

2 tablespoons heavy whipping cream

pinch of ground cinnamon

pinch of ground nutmeg

pinch of ground ginger

pinch of ground cloves

1. Combine all the ingredients in a small bowl and stir with a fork until combined.

2. When baked goods are still slightly warm, use a spoon to place a healthy dollop of glaze on each one. Spread the glaze around with the back of the spoon. Sprinkle with sugar, and allow the glaze to set for at least 1 hour.

CREAM CHEESE FROSTING

A tasty twist on a classic.

½ cup (1 stick) unsalted butter, at room temperature

8 ounces cream cheese, at room temperature

2 tablespoons pure molasses (optional, depending on what you're using it for)

4 tablespoons powdered sugar

1. In an electric mixer fitted with the paddle attachment, beat the butter and cream cheese on medium until combined.

2. Add the molasses, if using. Gradually add the powdered sugar. Spread on the desired baked good with a spatula.

SWEET TIPS:
Molasses is MAGIC. Buy the real stuff, though.

CONVERSIONS

MEASURE	EQUIVALENT	METRIC
1 teaspoon	--	5.0 milliliters
1 tablespoon	3 teaspoons	14.8 milliliters
1 cup	16 tablespoons	236.8 milliliters
1 pint	2 cups	473.6 milliliters
1 quart	4 cups	947.2 milliliters
1 liter	4 cups + 3½ tablespoons	1000 milliliters
1 ounce (dry)	2 tablespoons	28.35 grams
1 pound	16 ounces	453.49 grams
2.21 pounds	35.3 ounces	1 kilogram
325°F/350°F/375°F	--	165°C/177°C/190°C

ACKNOWLEDGMENTS

Mini thanks!

To our mini fans and followers. To our incredible families, friends, and fellow dessert lovers. We wouldn't have accomplished this little feat, or any of the ones prior to it, without the overwhelming support of the beloved people around us. Thanks to those willing to taste baked goods (no matter how homely) and provide honest feedback. Thanks to those willing to accommodate baker's hours. Thanks to our publisher for having as much faith in us as we did. Thanks to our mothers and grandmothers for instilling in us the basic truth that baking is love. We are lucky, humbled, and grateful for your encouragement. You know who you are.

ABOUT THE AUTHORS

MORGAN GREENSETH has been involved with the many aspects of food throughout her life. Growing up in the Midwest, as a young girl she learned to bake with her mother and grandmother. She now designs the interiors of restaurants and cafés, and also helps fill their pastry cases with treats. When not brightening up interiors, she's veganizing her favorite desserts and competing in baking competitions. She has written about food and the environment for www.worldchanging.com and has served as a panelist for the Fearless Critic Seattle Restaurant Guide book. Having relocated from Seattle, Washington, to New York City, Morgan now manages Champs diner and bakery.

CHRISTY BEAVER was raised in southern Arkansas and began helping her mother and grandmother in the kitchen as soon as she could walk, and quickly developed a lifelong love for pie. After moving to the Pacific Northwest, she noticed a lack of wholesome home-baked goods, which inspired her to start Mini Empire Bakery—she now heads up it's Seattle operations. In her spare time, Christy enjoys distance running and baking competitions. Her goals are to enable everyone to enjoy small portions of their favorite treats and to help Mini Empire take over the world, one tiny dessert at a time. She lives in Seattle, Washington, with her devoted dachshund, Andy.